CRIMINAL JUSTICE, LAW ENFORCEMENT AND CORRECTIONS

ORGANIZED CRIME, GANGS AND TRAFFICKING

CRIMINAL JUSTICE, LAW ENFORCEMENT AND CORRECTIONS

Additional books in this series can be found on Nova's website under the Series tab.

Additional E-books in this series can be found on Nova's website under the E-books tab.

CRIMINAL JUSTICE, LAW ENFORCEMENT AND CORRECTIONS

ORGANIZED CRIME, GANGS AND TRAFFICKING

CARTER M. WEBB
AND
PAUL W. DOBREV
EDITORS

Nova Science Publishers, Inc.
New York

For permission to use material from this book please contact us:
Telephone 631-231-7269; Fax 631-231-8175
Web Site: http://www.novapublishers.com

Additional color graphics may be available in the e-book version of this book.

LIBRARY OF CONGRESS CATALOGING-IN-PUBLICATION DATA

Organized crime, gangs and trafficking / editors, Carter M. Webb and Paul W. Dobrev.
p. cm. -- (Criminal justice, law enforcement and corrections)
Includes bibliographical references and index.
ISBN 978-1-61122-829-8 (alk. paper)
1. Organized crime--United States. 2. Human trafficking--China--Hong Kong. I. Webb, Carter M. II. Dobrev, Paul W.
HV6446.O757 2011
364.1'060973--dc22
2010044735

Published by Nova Science Publishers, Inc. † New York

CONTENTS

PREFACE

This book presents and discusses information in the study of organized crime, gangs and trafficking on a global scale. Topics discussed include organized crime in the U.S.; Taiwan and Hong Kong gangs; trafficking of mainland Chinese women to Taiwan; Hong Kong drug trafficking and human smuggling.

Chapter 1 - Organized crime threatens multiple facets of the United States, including the economy and national security. In fact, the Organized Crime Council was recently reconvened for the first time in 15 years to address this continued threat. Organized crime has taken on an increasingly transnational nature, and with more open borders and the expansion of the Internet, criminals endanger the United States not only from within the borders, but beyond. Threats come from a variety of criminal organizations, including Russian, Asian, Italian, Balkan, Middle Eastern, and African syndicates. Policymakers may question whether the tools they have provided the federal government to combat organized crime are still effective for countering today's evolving risks.

In the wake of the economic downturn, organized crime could further weaken the economy with illegal activities (such as cigarette trafficking and tax evasion scams) that result in a loss of tax revenue for state and federal governments. Fraudulent activities in domains such as strategic commodities, credit, insurance, stocks, securities and investments could further weaken the already-troubled financial market.

On the national security front, experts and policymakers have expressed concern over a possible nexus between organized crime and terrorism. Despite the difference in motivation for organized crime (profit) and terrorism (ideology), the linking element for the two is money. Terrorists may potentially obtain funding for their operations from partnering directly with organized crime groups or modeling their profitable criminal acts. Even if organized crime groups and terrorist organizations do not form long-term alliances, the possibility of short-term business alliances may be of concern to policymakers.

In light of these developments, several possible issues for Congress arise. One issue centers on whether the evolving nature of organized crime requires new enforcement tools. Some policymakers have suggested that current laws may not be effective at countering present threats from organized crime. As organized criminals threaten American society from both within and outside U.S. borders, should Congress expand law enforcement's extraterritorial jurisdiction to investigate and prosecute these criminals, and to what extent should Congress encourage multilateral—both domestic and international—crime fighting efforts? Legislation has been introduced in the 111th Congress (H.R. 1793, S. 49, S. 378, and S. 386, for example) that would expand the list of predicate offenses under the Racketeer Influenced and Corrupt Organizations Act (RICO), clarify the definition of money laundering, and expand the international money laundering statute.

Another possible issue for Congress concerns whether the resources that the federal government allocates to organized crime matters are adequate and appropriately allocated to counter the threats it poses. Following the terrorist attacks of September 11, 2001, national priorities and federal resources shifted away from more traditional crime fighting—including that of organized crime—toward counterterrorism and counterintelligence. For instance, the number of federal agents actually working on organized crime matters and the number of organized crime cases opened in FY2004 decreased relative to levels before September 11, 2001. This report will be updated as needed.

Chapter 2 - One thing we have learned from our recent interviews and research in Asia is that it is very hard to generalize about the problem of organized crime there. For example, there is little consensus among law enforcement authorities as to what the leading organized crime problems in Asia are. Nevertheless, if we are to try to generalize, our impression is that local law enforcement authorities in Asia seem to be more focused on traditional organized crime activities such as extortion, gambling, prostitution, loan sharking, debt-collection, and violence than they are on transnational organized crime activities such as drug trafficking, human smuggling /trafficking, arms trafficking, and money laundering. Moreover, many Asian officials are concerned with the nexus between gangsters and politicians, and especially the penetration of organized crime figures into business and politics.

In this section, we will first briefly discuss some of the most important organized crime problems in the eight research sites, according to the information we received from our interviews with local authorities. We will then examine the viewpoint of American officials in Asia, and close by adding our own assessment. By traditional organized crime groups we mean groups that have continuity across crimes and over time, that engage in multiple criminal enterprises, that employ violence and corruption, and that usually have hierarchical structures.

Chapter 3 - There are many crime groups in Asia, some of them indigenous and others imported from abroad or formed by foreigners. As with the task of ranking the seriouness of organized crime problems in Asia, the attempt to generalize the scope of each and every organized crime group is also difficult because this may depend on the country, the group, and the product or service involved.

Chapter 4 - As a description and illustration of the impact of Asian organized criminality on the United States, it is important to point out what the authors' discussion does and does not contain. In the latter category, they do not deal with the garden variety of crimes that just happen to have been committed by Asians, nor do they examine the Asian street gangs that operate in certain U.S. cities. Instead, the authors' focus is first upon those crimes that appear to be transnational in nature – the U.S. being on the receiving end – and, that originate in (or at least involve) any of the eight countries (or administrative regions) that were the focal point of their study here. They realize that any gaps in their coverage may be in part a consequence of these choices.

The second focus requires that the authors construe impact and harm broadly, to include not only direct criminal activities in the United States, but also harm and/or potential harm to U.S. interests both at home and abroad. For example, given the history and the volatility of relations between mainland China and Taiwan, and the strong U.S. interest and investment in that area, criminal developments involving those entities are of critical interest to the United States. In other cases, where there are developing U.S. business interests, such as in China and in the casino industry in Macau, again there is the potential for a criminal impact on U.S. interests. Such matters are our second focus.

The methods the authors employed in their research clearly influence their ability to discern the threat, impact, and harm to the U.S. and to U.S. interests, and thus a further word about methodology is in order. As noted, their principal respondents in interviews were nationals (scholars, law enforcement officials, and in some cases victims) of the respective countries that were visited. Thus, the authors' perspective of how, what they know, might impact upon the United States is pretty much speculative. Even in the cases of the U.S. officials that were interviewed in each country, their perspectives on the crime and organized crime problems are an "in-country" view, albeit keeping United States' interests very much in mind.

In addition to the interviews and field visits that were conducted, as previously mentioned, local scholars in Hong Kong and Taiwan prepared market assessments of the criminal markets of human trafficking and drug trafficking, and also analyses of the major organized crime groups in each of their respective areas. Again, we should recognize that these reflect the perspectives of those native scholars.

None of this should be construed to mean that the interviews, assessments, and analyses are not valuable – quite to the contrary. The original sources provide a foundation, a stepping off point, to compare and relate what was learned from them, with a plethora of existing secondary materials. We will therefore look at what the authors learned in the context of what has been recently reported in various U.S. government reports and research studies. The latter include in particular: (1) the U.S. State Department's Trafficking in Persons Report for 2004; (2) "The Commercial Sexual Exploitation of Children in the U.S., Canada and Mexico" (a 2002 report to NIJ by Estes and Weiner); (3) "Sex Trafficking of Women in the United States" (a 2001 report to NIJ by Raymond and Hughes); and (4) a "Survey of Practitioners to Assess the Local Impact of Transnational Crime" (a 2003 report to NIJ by Abt Associates). The authors also look to the work of Bertil Linter in his 2002 book, Blood Brothers: The Criminal Underworld in Asia.

Chapter 5 - The Bamboo United has a headquarters and numerous local branches. According to a 1985 sentencing report, the headquarters is made up of an "Ultimate Gang Leader" (or "Headquarters' Leader" or "Boss"), an "Ultimate Enforcer," and an "Ultimate Superintendent." Various police reports have also suggested that there is an "Ultimate Executive" in the headquarters. The Ultimate Gang Leader leads the gang, the Ultimate Enforcer enforces gang rules, the Ultimate Superintendent monitors gang members and their activities, and the Ultimate Executive operates gang businesses. In 1981, the gang established its first eight branches: Chung (loyalty), Shao (filial pity), Len (sympathy), Eia (love), Shing (trust), Yi (righteousness), Hor (harmony), and Ping (peace). By 1996, there were 21 branches and currently there are more than 60 branches. A branch or a tong has a Branch Leader, Deputy Branch Leader, and "brothers" (or members). Some branches (such as the Ho

Tong) also have a Right-arm Enforcer, Left-arm Enforcer, Communication Officer, War Officer, and Internal Regulator. Recently, some branches have had their own sub-branches and some of the sub-branches are "guardian unit" or "combat unit" in nature. Even though there are many branches in the Bamboo United, most of these branches are located in urban centers, especially Taipei City and Taipei County. Branches are often involved in intra-gang conflicts; for example, Ho Tong and Sky Dragon Tong have fought over debt-collection; and Air Tong and Heaven and Earth Tong got involved in a nasty war as a result of a minor argument.

Chapter 6 - According to police records, only 14 out of the 50 triad societies remain active in Hong Kong. Out of these 14 active groups, San Yee One is regarded as one of the most influential triad groups. It was originally formed by a Chinese minority native group called Chiu Chau in Hong Kong. Nowadays members of San Yee On come from different ethnic Chinese groups. A small number of local born Indian and Pakistan are also recruited to the Society. Nevertheless, San Yee On is still a male dominant secret society. Few females joined the Society formally.

Chapter 7 - According to statistical data released on March 31, 2004 by the National Police Administration (NPA), 2,345 illegal immigrants from China were arrested in the year 2003. The number of arrested illegal immigrants has increased by 28% (512) over 2002. Among the arrestees, 1,001 people (43%) said they were not employed yet at the time of their arrests, 894 people (38%) admitted they were working as prostitutes, and 418 people (18%) said they were illegally employed. In 2003, it was the first time that illegal female immigrants (1,962) outnumbered illegal male immigrants, a result of a 41% (569) increase from the previous year. Among the female immigrants, 894 said they were sex workers, 840 indicated they were not yet employed. Among female immigrants, 1,233 (36%) were between the age of 16 and 20, which is the largest age group. There were 1,095 (32%) women between the age of 21 and 25, which is the second largest age group. There were 521 (15%) women between the age of 26 to 30, which is the third largest age group. In sum, most illegal immigrants from China were young females.

The majority of the illegal immigrants were arrested in three different areas: the coastal area, inland, and on the sea. Over the years, most illegal immigrants were arrested inland. In inland areas, 2,603 people were arrested in 2003, an increase of 44% (797) from 2002. Among them, police arrested 1,845 (71%) people, mostly in Taipei City, Taipei County, Taoyuan County and Taichung City. There were 754 (29%) illegal immigrants arrested by the Coast Guard Administration. Three hundred and fifty illegal immigrants were arrested on the water in 2003, a decrease of 27% (127) from the previous year. All of those were apprehended by officers from the Coast Guard Administration. On March 31, 2004, there were 2,155 illegal immigrants being detained in various detention centers exclusively for Mainland Chinese. Among them 1,132 people were detained in the center in Yilan, 1,011 people in the center in Hsinchu, and 12 people in the center in Matsu.

Chapter 8 - In 2003, a high priority was again accorded to tackling psychotropic substance abuse. Police were able to consolidate on the success in the previous year in reducing the problem. When compared to 2002 there was a 25% decrease in the number of young persons arrested in respect of psychotropic substance cases. Throughout the year police made every effort to cut-off the supply of psychotropic substances to the mainly young abusers. During numerous enforcement operations, various police units joined forces to enhance the effectiveness in quelling the psychotropic substance problem.

The heroin reaching the Hong Kong, Special Administrative Region (SAR) invariably originates from the Golden Triangle. The heroin is smuggled overland through Mainland China to clandestine stores in areas of southern China adjacent to the SAR. Hong Kong syndicates arrange for numerous small amounts of heroin to be smuggled into Hong Kong via the land boundary with the Mainland. The sheer volume of traffic coming through the boundary provides opportunities for traffickers to avoid detection. As Hong Kong is not used as a significant drug transit centre nowadays, heroin smuggled into the SAR is for local abusers. At the start of the year heroin divans (premises where addicts go to purchase and consume the narcotic) were a major focus of attention for police. The majority were situated in the Kowloon West Region. Numerous operations to neutralize the divans resulted in a substantial reduction in such premises operating towards the end of the year.

Three heroin-cutting centres were dismantled in 2003. Arrests in relation to heroin offences were down by around 5.2% when compared to the previous year. A total of 52.87 KGs kilograms of heroin were seized.

The average wholesale price of heroin in 2003 was HK$256,638 per kilogram, an increase when compared to the average wholesale price HK$222,592 in 2002. The average retail price of heroin increased from HK$419.91 per gram in 2002 to HK$424.75 per gram in 2003. Retail purity increased to an average of 59% when compared to an average purity of 41.5% in 2002.

Ketamine seizures and arrests were again relatively high in 2003. The drug has now become firmly established as the most prevalent drug of abuse among young persons in the SAR. The abuse of ketamine was inextricably linked to the still popular rave/dance party music scene in the SAR. With a diminishing number of dance parties held in large hired venues, abuse tended to be in discos, bars, karaoke lounges or in private settings. The number of persons arrested for offences related to ketamine in 2003 was 1,770, a fall of 24.9% on the preceding year. In 2003, the average wholesale price of ketamine was HK$57,125 per kilogram and the average retail price was HK$194 per gram.

Again in 2003, as seen in recent years, there were tablets in circulation, being sold to consumers as "ecstasy", that were found to contain a mixture of dangerous drugs. Many tablets seized contained a mix of ketamine and methamphetamine. Those tablets that contained MDMA, the substance originally associated with the term ecstasy, were found to contain a wide variation in the volume of the active ingredient. In some tablets the MDMA content was as low as 70 mg, in others it was more than double at around 150 mg per tablet. Ecstasy-type tablets are brought into Hong Kong from production sources by couriers. Packages of the small (roughly 8mm diameter) tablets are taped to the body and hidden under clothing or concealed in luggage. The retail price of an ecstasy-type tablet decreased from around HK$90 in 2002 to around HK$85 in 2003. Over the year, a total of 141,038 ecstasy-type tablets were seized, an almost three-fold increase when compared with 48,840 tablets seized in 2002. The increase can be ascribed to three major cases where several thousands of tablets were seized. In a significant case, a fairly sophisticated ecstasy-type tablet production enterprise based in Kowloon was dismantled.

Passengers concealing small quantities on their person or in luggage bring cannabis from the Golden Triangle and Cambodia into the SAR. Larger consignments may be smuggled by the sea route. The total herbal cannabis seizures for the year amounted to 586.61 kilograms. The average wholesale price of herbal cannabis decreased to about HK$16,083 per kilogram in 2003 as compared to average wholesale price of HK$16,396 per kilogram in 2002. The average retail price of herbal cannabis decreased slightly from HK$67 per gram in 2002 to HK$58 in 2003. The amount of cannabis resin seized increased substantially from 0.37 kilograms in 2002 to 24.46 kilograms in 2003.

Methamphetamine, in crystalline form or sometimes liquid form, is smuggled into the SAR via the land boundary with the Mainland. Whilst the vast majority is for local consumption, in a few cases foreign nationals from Asia have been apprehended when attempting to smuggle small amounts of 'ice' back to their homelands via the Hong Kong International Airport. In 2003, a total of 41.10 kilograms of methamphetamine were seized. The wholesale price of methamphetamine averaged HK$54,458 per kilogram in 2003 while the average retail price of one gram was HK$374

Cocaine, originating from South America, is smuggled into Hong Kong by couriers secreting the drug on their body or in luggage and sometimes by swallowing the drug. Another method of smuggling cocaine is to send it to the SAR by post or courier falsely declared as some innocuous item. In 2003, cocaine remained expensive with an average retail price of HK$1,152 per gram. The logistics of trafficking cocaine from distant production areas in South America to the region and consequent limited supply keep the costs high. Cocaine abuse has not been widespread in the SAR. The total cocaine seizures in 2003 amounted to 8.33 kilograms, a slight increase compared to 8.30 kilograms in 2002.

Abuse of prescription medicinal preparations continued in 2003 and seizures of midazolam (38,617 tablets), chlordiazepoxide (24,784 tablets), diazepam (22,190 tablets) and triazolam (13,165 tablets) were made. Young persons often abuse tranquillizers, however, heroin addicts also consume the tablets to prolong the effect of the narcotic and ease withdrawal symptoms. A relatively new drug of abuse to Hong Kong with the proprietary name 'Erimin 5' which contains Nimetazepam, was abused by youngsters along with other psychotropic substances in 2003.

On one occasion in 2003 a small amount of Gamma-Hydroxybutyric Acid (GHB) was seized. This was the fourth seizure of the drug in Hong Kong since it was scheduled as a dangerous drug in October 2001.

In order to interdict transnational drug trafficking the Hong Kong Police and Customs officers work closely with their counterparts in the Mainland and overseas. As a result of the close partnership with Mainland enforcement agencies, substantial seizures of drugs were made before the illicit consignments could reach lower level traffickers and abusers. Furthermore, Narcotics Bureau of the Police participated in several major international drug trafficking investigations with overseas law-enforcement agencies in 2003. Significant seizures made overseas with the assistance of Narcotics Bureau totaled 92 kgs of methamphetamine, 9.3 kgs of heroin, 800 kgs of cannabis and 12,000 ecstasy-type tablets.

Chapter 9 - In law enforcement community, the terms ‘human smuggling’ and ‘illegal migration’ are used interchangeably though there is a distinct difference in their nature.

Human smuggling is commonly understood as the process in which a person physically participates for gaining illegal entry into a country. There are a variety of reasons that initiate that person to set off his illicit attempt but his final goal is no more than making a decisive intent for migration to the receiving country.

Hence, human smuggling is the prerequisite process that leads to the fulfillment of one's intent for illegal migration. Alternatively speaking, human smuggling is the means and illegal migration is the goal.

Versions of these chapters were also published in *Journal of Current Issues in Crime, Law and Law Enforcement* Volume 1, Numbers 3-4, and Volume 2, Number 1, published by Nova Science Publishers, Inc. They were submitted for appropriate modifications in an effort to encourage wider dissemination of research.

In: Organized Crime, Gangs and Trafficking ISBN: 978-1-61122-829-8
Editors: C. Webb and P. Dobrev

Chapter 1

ORGANIZED CRIME IN THE UNITED STATES: TRENDS AND ISSUES FOR CONGRESS*

Kristin M. Finklea#

ABSTRACT

Organized crime threatens multiple facets of the United States, including the economy and national security. In fact, the Organized Crime Council was recently reconvened for the first time in 15 years to address this continued threat. Organized crime has taken on an increasingly transnational nature, and with more open borders and the expansion of the Internet, criminals endanger the United States not only from within the borders, but beyond. Threats come from a variety of criminal organizations, including Russian, Asian, Italian, Balkan, Middle Eastern, and African syndicates. Policymakers may question whether the tools they have provided the federal government to combat organized crime are still effective for countering today's evolving risks.

In the wake of the economic downturn, organized crime could further weaken the economy with illegal activities (such as cigarette trafficking and tax evasion scams) that result in a loss of tax revenue for state and federal governments. Fraudulent activities in domains such as strategic

* This is an edited, reformatted and augmented version of CRS Report R40525 dated April 16, 2009.

E-mail: kfinklea@crs.loc.gov

commodities, credit, insurance, stocks, securities and investments could further weaken the already-troubled financial market.

On the national security front, experts and policymakers have expressed concern over a possible nexus between organized crime and terrorism. Despite the difference in motivation for organized crime (profit) and terrorism (ideology), the linking element for the two is money. Terrorists may potentially obtain funding for their operations from partnering directly with organized crime groups or modeling their profitable criminal acts. Even if organized crime groups and terrorist organizations do not form long-term alliances, the possibility of short-term business alliances may be of concern to policymakers.

In light of these developments, several possible issues for Congress arise. One issue centers on whether the evolving nature of organized crime requires new enforcement tools. Some policymakers have suggested that current laws may not be effective at countering present threats from organized crime. As organized criminals threaten American society from both within and outside U.S. borders, should Congress expand law enforcement's extraterritorial jurisdiction to investigate and prosecute these criminals, and to what extent should Congress encourage multilateral—both domestic and international—crime fighting efforts? Legislation has been introduced in the 111th Congress (H.R. 1793, S. 49, S. 378, and S. 386, for example) that would expand the list of predicate offenses under the Racketeer Influenced and Corrupt Organizations Act (RICO), clarify the definition of money laundering, and expand the international money laundering statute.

Another possible issue for Congress concerns whether the resources that the federal government allocates to organized crime matters are adequate and appropriately allocated to counter the threats it poses. Following the terrorist attacks of September 11, 2001, national priorities and federal resources shifted away from more traditional crime fighting—including that of organized crime—toward counterterrorism and counterintelligence. For instance, the number of federal agents actually working on organized crime matters and the number of organized crime cases opened in FY2004 decreased relative to levels before September 11, 2001. This report will be updated as needed.

INTRODUCTION

Organized crime threatens the economy, national security, and other interests of the United States [1]. Particularly in the past several decades, organized crime has been evolving and taking on an increasingly transnational nature. With more open borders and the expansion of the Internet, organized criminals threaten the United States not only from within the borders, but beyond. Organized crime stretches far beyond the Italian mafia, encompassing Russian, Asian, Balkan, Middle Eastern, and African syndicates. Even though organized crime has not received as much recent media or congressional attention as have other national concerns, such as the threat of terrorism, these criminals have not ceased their illicit activities.

Illustrating that the threats from organized crime remain, former Attorney General Michael Mukasey reconvened the Organized Crime Council (OCC) in April 2008 to address the evolving threats from organized crime [2]. Beyond the individual illegal activities committed by organized crime groups (e.g., gambling, prostitution, labor racketeering, smuggling/trafficking, extortion, theft, murder, and money laundering), the OCC has indicated that these organizations may:

- penetrate the energy and other strategic sectors of the economy;
- provide logistical and other support to terrorists, foreign intelligence services, and governments;
- smuggle/traffic people and contraband goods into the United States;
- exploit the United States and international financial system to move illicit funds;
- use cyberspace to target U.S. victims and infrastructure;
- manipulate securities exchanges and perpetrate sophisticated frauds;
- corrupt or seek to corrupt public officials in the United States and abroad; and
- use violence or the threat of violence as a basis for power.

The domestic impact from the activities of organized crime groups thus extends beyond what many may consider to be traditional organized crime activities. Congress may wish to consider the impact of organized crime on domestic issues of immediate concern, such as the economy and national security. Do these evolving threats from organized crime require new tools to combat it?

Another issue that the 111th Congress may wish to consider is the adequacy of the resources the federal government allocates to organized crime. Following the terrorist attacks of September 11, 2001, national priorities and federal resources shifted away from more traditional crime fighting—including that of organized crime—toward counterterrorism and counterintelligence. Subsequently, there has been a decrease in the federal law enforcement resources dedicated to organized crime matters and a decrease in the number of federal organized crime cases opened [3]

Consequently, the policy question facing Congress is, Are the resources that the federal government allocates to organized crime matters sufficient to counter the threats that organized crime pose?

This report provides a background on organized crime in the United States as well as the tools that Congress has afforded for the federal government to combat it. It outlines the trends in federal efforts to investigate and prosecute organized crime. The report then discusses the evolving nature of organized crime, including the domestic impact of organized crime, prominent organized crime groups, and their illegal activities affecting the United States. It concludes with a discussion of issues that the 111th Congress may wish to consider, including the attention the federal government allocates to organized crime matters, the multilateral efforts to combat organized crime, and issues surrounding a potential nexus between organized crime and terrorism.

DEFINITIONS OF ORGANIZED CRIME

A clear definition of organized crime is important for both legal and policy purposes. Some experts suggest that although organized crime is difficult to define, the various attributes of criminal organizations are central to the definition. This report uses the attributes of a criminal organization, in combination with the definitions of organized crime, enterprise, and racketeering as outlined in the current law, as a framework for discussing the trends in organized crime and policy issues for Congress to consider.

Specifically, attributes of organized crime may involve:

- structure,
- restricted membership,
- continuity,
- violence or the threat of violence,
- illegal enterprises,
- legitimate business penetration,
- corruption, and
- lack of ideology [4]

The structure of modern organized crime groups often does not exhibit the rigid hierarchy of more traditional organized crime groups such as the Italian Mafia [5]. Moreover, organized crime groups restrict membership based on a number of factors, including race, ethnicity, kinship, and criminal background.

These criminal organizations continue, even if leadership or membership changes over time. Further, violence and/or the threat of violence are integral aspects of organized crime. Organized crime groups profit from illegal enterprises as well as from infiltrating legitimate businesses. They may attempt to corrupt public officials in order to escape investigation, prosecution, or punishment. Notably, the primary goal of organized crime groups is to make money; these groups are profit-driven rather than ideology-driven (a key distinction between organized crime and terrorist groups) [6]

Statutory Definition

The statutory definition of organized crime stems from the Omnibus Crime Control and Safe Streets Act of 1968, as amended (P.L. 90-351). Current law defines organized crime as "the unlawful activities of the members of a highly organized, disciplined association engaged in supplying illegal goods and services, including but not limited to gambling, prostitution, loan sharking, narcotics, labor racketeering, and other unlawful activities of members of such organizations." This definition describes organized crime in terms of the illegal activities rather than in terms of what constitutes a criminal organization. In the Organized Crime Control Act of 1970 (P.L. 91-452), and more specifically within Title IX—the Racketeer Influenced and Corrupt Organizations Act (RICO) [7] — organized crime is defined in terms of an "enterprise" and a "pattern of racketeering activity." [8]. The predicate offenses for racketeering include a host of state and federal crimes listed in 18 U.S.C. § 1961. Although RICO provides a definition for an "enterprise," it does not describe the attributes of a criminal enterprise that distinguish it from a legal enterprise. In addition, this definition describes organized crime more in terms of the illegal activities than in terms of the criminal organization.

BACKGROUND

Organized crime in the United States has a long-standing history. Although this history has its origins prior to the 20th century, organized crime flourished around the time of Prohibition [9] and grabbed the attention of policymakers. Through most of the 20th century, U.S. law enforcement combated what most consider "traditional" organized crime networks operating inside the United States, including the Italian Mafia, Russian Mafia,

Japanese Yakuza, and Chinese Tongs. These criminal organizations were involved in a variety of illegal activities, and in the 195 0s and 1960s, the most profitable of these activities was gambling, followed by loan sharking, narcotics trafficking, extortion, prostitution, bootlegging, and fraud [10]. Other prominent activities of organized crime groups were racketeering, theft, murder, and money laundering.

The national focus on organized crime led to several efforts aimed at investigating and controlling it. These initial efforts included the Senate Special Committee to Investigate Organized Crime in Interstate Commerce in 1950 and 1951 led by Senator Kefauver, Senate hearings on organized crime in 1958 and 1963 led by Senator McClellan, [11] a series of conferences on organized crime at Oyster Bay in 1965 and 1966, and the creation of the 1967 Task Force on Organized Crime. This 1967 Task Force reported that law enforcement measures to curb organized crime had not been successful [12] and, further, that organized crime in America was on the rise [13] Statistics showed that from 1961 to 1966, the number of individuals indicted by the Organized Crime and Racketeering Section (OCRS) of the Department of Justice (DOJ) rose from 121 to 1,198. Further, the number of those indicted individuals actually convicted rose from 73 to 477 [14]. Although the raw number of indictments and convictions rose between 1961 and 1966, CRS analysis revealed that the proportion of individuals from organized crime groups who were convicted during this period actually declined, from 60.3% to 39.8% [15]

Combating organized crime had been a responsibility primarily of state and local law enforcement.16 As the scope of organized crime was continuing to increase, Congress recognized the need for better crime fighting tools and the need to further the federal government's role in fighting and prosecuting organized crime [17].

Omnibus Crime Control and Safe Streets Act

One of the first steps taken by Congress to increase the federal government's role in combating organized crime included a series of congressional hearings in 1967 and 1968 and the enactment of the Omnibus Crime Control and Safe Streets Act of 1968 (P.L. 90-351). The Omnibus Crime Control and Safe Streets Act of 1968 was one of the first major pieces of legislation to directly address organized crime. Specifically, it provided grant money via the Law Enforcement Assistance Administration (LEAA)

[18] to state law enforcement agencies to combat organized crime. Included in the Act was the congressional finding that

> organized criminals make extensive use of wire and oral communications in their criminal activities. The interception of such communications to obtain evidence of the commission of crimes or to prevent their commission is an indispensable aid to law enforcement and the administration of justice.

Title III of this Act permitted federal law enforcement agencies to wiretap conversations of suspected criminals, including suspects of organized crime [19]. Electronic wiretapping authority granted in the Omnibus Crime Control and Safe Streets Act of 1968 immediately provided American law enforcement and policymakers with an indication of organized criminals' activity, specifically their involvement in illegally importing and distributing narcotics.20 Despite these tools to combat criminals, the federal government still lacked the tools to combat criminal organizations [21]

The Organized Crime Control Act and RICO

The Organized Crime Control Act of 1970 (P.L. 91-452) strengthened the ability of the federal government to combat and prosecute criminal organizations. It provided for Special Grand Juries to investigate multi jurisdictional organized crime; these grand juries are able to produce reports outlining public corruption and organized crime conditions in their respective districts. The Act also allowed for witnesses of organized crime to be granted immunity from prosecution in exchange for testimony. Further, it authorized security for government witnesses or potential witnesses in organized crime cases. This measure laid the groundwork for the Witness Security Program (WITSEC) [22]. The WITSEC program allows for the protection and relocation of witnesses and their families, whose lives may be in danger as a result of their testimony in organized and other major crime cases.

Title IX of the Organized Crime Control Act of 1970 created the Racketeer Influenced and Corrupt Organizations Act (RICO) [23]. Many view RICO as the single most important piece of organized crime legislation enacted [24]. RICO allows for the prosecution of anyone who participates or conspires to participate in a criminal enterprise/organization through two acts of "racketeering activity" within a 10-year period of time. The predicate offenses for racketeering include various state and federal crimes listed in the

U.S. Code [25]. Since its enactment, RICO has been one of the dominant tools used in organized crime prosecutions.

Asset Forfeiture and Money Laundering Statutes

Since the passage of RICO, Congress has enacted legislation regarding asset forfeiture and money laundering, both of which have increased the federal government's ability to combat organized crime [26]. The asset forfeiture and money laundering statutes have provided a means for the federal government to further attack the financial structure and assets of organized crime groups [27]. Although RICO included provisions for asset forfeiture, the Comprehensive Crime Control Act of 1984 (P.L. 98-473) expanded upon these provisions. Specifically, Title II of Chapter III—the Comprehensive Forfeiture Act of 1984—amended RICO by specifying that proceeds (both tangible and intangible) obtained directly or indirectly from racketeering activity were subject to forfeiture. This Act also established the Department of Justice's Asset Forfeiture Fund in the Department of the Treasury. The rules for civil forfeiture proceedings were later revised in the Civil Asset Forfeiture Reform Act of 2000 (P.L. 106-185), improving the federal government's ability to prosecute organized crime cases. Money laundering, the primary method of concealing the illicit proceeds from organized crime activities or placing them back into further illegal activity, was established as a federal criminal offense in the Money Laundering Control Act of 1986 (P.L. 99-570) [28] This Act also established criminal and civil penalties for money laundering, as well as procedures for forfeiting the illicit funds. It appears that these laws have all provided effective tools, as the Department of Justice and Federal Bureau of Investigation have indicated that the three most prominent tools relied upon when investigating and prosecuting organized crime are RICO, money laundering, and asset forfeiture statutes.

More Recent Federal Attention to Organized Crime [29]

Following the terrorist attacks of September 11, 2001, congressional and national law enforcement priorities shifted away from traditional crime fighting toward counterterrorism. More recently, however, there appears to be an increase in national attention to the need for fighting more traditional crime, including organized crime [30]. In fact, after a 15-year hiatus, the Organized Crime Council met in April 2008 for the first time since 1993.31 The renewed attention to traditional crime fighting—and specifically for purposes of this discussion, organized crime— has increasingly shifted toward the transnational nature of organized crime. Though organized crime has arguably always been transnational, it was not until the 1990s, following the Cold War and the spread of globalization, that the transnational nature of organized crime surged and criminals expanded their operations across increasingly open borders.

Federal Law Enforcement Efforts to Combat Organized Crime

In general, domestic crime control tends to fall on the shoulders of state and local law enforcement agencies. As mentioned above, however, the federal government began to play a larger role in combating organized crime following the enactment of the Omnibus Crime Control and Safe Streets Act of 1968, and even more after RICO and the Organized Crime Control Act of 1970. Various federal agencies are currently involved in controlling the activities of organized crime groups. In addition to domestic efforts to combat organized crime, the federal government is also involved in international efforts.

Domestic Efforts

Combating organized crime is not a task handled by one federal agency or even one department. Many agencies have a hand in tackling the threats posed by organized crime. The Department of Justice, specifically the U.S. Attorney General's Organized Crime Council, is responsible for creating domestic organized crime policy [32]. The Council is chaired by the Deputy Attorney General and has representatives from the Federal Bureau of Investigation (FBI); the U.S. Drug Enforcement Agency (DEA); the Bureau of Alcohol, Tobacco, Firearms and Explosives (ATF); the U.S. Immigration and Customs Enforcement (ICE); the U.S. Secret Service; the Internal Revenue Service (IRS); the U.S. Postal Inspection Service; Diplomatic Security; and the U.S. Department of Labor, Office of the Inspector General.

Although many federal and state departments and agencies are involved in fighting organized crime, the primary agency responsible for combating organized crime is the FBI [33]. The Transnational Criminal Enterprise

Section in the Criminal Enterprise Branch of the Criminal Investigative Division is responsible for investigating organized crime. This Organized Crime Section is divided into three principal units investigating (1) La Cosa Nostra, Italian organized crime, and racketeering; (2) Eurasian/Middle Eastern organized crime; and (3) Asian and African criminal enterprises [34]

As its key analytical tool, the FBI uses the Enterprise Theory of Investigation (ETI) to investigate organized crime. ETI involves two steps: (1) identifying a criminal organization and the criminal activities of this organization and (2) identifying the financial assets of the criminal organization for possible forfeiture [35]. This investigative technique seems to complement the RICO statutes in that both ETI and RICO are aimed at dismantling criminal organizations. Further, ETI identifies financial assets that may be subject to forfeiture under civil RICO statutes. This aspect of ETI is directed at combating money laundering and thus the financial lifeline of organized crime.

Domestic Working Groups and Task Forces [36]

Many of the FBI field offices have organized crime task forces. In those regions, the FBI works with state and local partners as well as with other federal agencies to combat organized crime. These task forces may be broader task forces covering a range of criminal syndicates, or they may be more specific covering a particular organized crime group. One example of a broad organized crime task force exists at the Minneapolis field division of the FBI; this division leads an Organized Crime Task Force that combines the efforts of other federal agencies as well as local law enforcement to target a number of criminal organizations involved in various crimes [37]. On the other hand, examples of more specific organized crime task forces exist at the FBI's New York division; in New York, there have been designated La Cosa Nostra (LCN) task forces, some dedicated to specific LCN families [38] Even if standing task forces are not formed, domestic agencies work jointly and rely on the resources of one another to combat organized crime. For example, when investigating labor racketeering, the FBI may work with the Department of Labor, the Department of Transportation, and the Internal Revenue Service, as well as state and local authorities.

With respect to prosecuting organized crime cases, the Department of Justice Organized Crime and Racketeering Section has Strike Force Units dedicated to organized crime. These units currently exist in U.S. Attorneys' Offices in 21 of the 93 federal districts with a large organized crime presence. The Strike Force Units operate in these particular 21 offices for historical reasons; those are the 21 offices where the LCN has had the largest presence, and the Strike Force Units continue to operate out of those offices. These units comprise a group of prosecutors with particular expertise in large, multi-defendant RICO cases [39]. Ultimately, the U.S. Attorney General is the chief law enforcement officer responsible for criminal investigations and prosecutions, including those of organized crime.

International Efforts

The United Nations Convention Against Transnational Organized Crime [40] is the main international tool for combating organized crime. In 2005, the United States ratified the Convention as well as the companion Protocols on trafficking in persons and smuggling of migrants. Among other provisions, the Convention provides for greater law enforcement cooperation and mutual legal assistance across nations where there were no previous agreements for such assistance. With the evolving transnational nature of organized crime, this coordination with international organizations is essential. Further, with increasingly open borders and the expansion of the Internet, organized criminals threaten American society not only from within the borders, but beyond.

One outcome of increasing transnational crime is that domestic federal law enforcement agencies work with international organizations to combat organized crime threats to the United States. As one example of this cooperation, the U.S. government and federal agencies support the United Nations (UN) Office of Drugs and Crime (UNODC) efforts to combat international organized crime. UNODC helps UN member countries implement provisions of the Convention Against Transnational Organized Crime to counter organized crime problems. Within the Department of Justice, the U.S. National Central Bureau (USNCB) of the International Criminal Police Organization (INTERPOL) [41] is the point of contact for INTERPOL matters in the United States. The USNCB can access INTERPOL's databases, and it coordinates requests for international investigations between U.S. law enforcement and their international partners [42]. Specifically, the USNCB Terrorism and Violent Crimes Division coordinates requests on organized crime cases. Also, the FBI participates in several international working groups and task forces to formulate best practices in combating organized crime.

International Working Groups and Task Forces

Federal law enforcement agencies in the United States and in Italy participate in the Italian American Working Group, which first met in 1984. This working group addresses problems common to both countries, including organized crime, drug trafficking, money laundering, cyber crime, and extradition issues. The Pantheon Project furthers the law enforcement relationship between the United States and Italy. The Project provides for two FBI agents that work at the Italian National Police headquarters and for two Italian officers that work at the FBI.

With respect to Russian organized crime, the FBI is involved in international working groups, including the Eurasian Organized Crime Working Group, the Central European Working Group, and the Southern European Cooperative Initiative. In addition, the FBI set up a joint FBI/Hungarian National Police task force in Budapest, Hungary, to combat Russian organized crime.43 This task force was established in 2000 to counter the increasing threat of Russian organized crime and is the only international task force in which the FBI is currently involved. The FBI has requested additional funding for this task force in its 2011-2015 budget. The FBI, in conjunction with other law enforcement agencies around the world, has also provided INTERPOL with information on individuals involved in Eurasian organized crime; this information is the basis for Project Millennium, a multinational effort, led by INTERPOL, to combat Eurasian organized crime.

Federal Investigations and Prosecutions of Organized Crime

According to the Department of Justice and the FBI, the threats posed by organized crime have become more broad and complex than ever before. Federal resources dedicated to organized crime matters, however, do not appear to have expanded along with the threats, and have actually decreased since 2001. After the September 11, 2001, terrorist attacks, national priorities, including those of federal law enforcement, shifted further toward counterterrorism-related activities and further away from traditional crime fighting activities. Within the law enforcement domain, this shift can be objectively seen in the field agents assigned to organized crime casework, the cases investigated, and the cases handled by the U.S. Attorneys' Offices.

Agent Utilization

Following the September 11, 2001, terrorist attacks, the FBI reorganized, prioritizing counterterrorism and counterintelligence over traditional crime matters. The FBI did not, however, significantly change its field agent allocation for organized crime matters between FY2001 and FY2004. Agent allocation remained nearly constant at 700, 697, 698, and 720 agents, respectively, for FY200 1 -FY2004 [44]. On the other hand, the FBI utilization of field agents in organized crime matters during this time period did not mirror that of the agent allocation. Figure 1 illustrates that the allocation of agents remained relatively constant, while the actual utilization decreased. The Department of Justice, Office of the Inspector General (OIG), found that in FY2004 the FBI utilized 35% fewer agents on organized crime matters than it did in FY2000.45 While the FBI utilized 682 agents on organized crime matters in FY2000, this number dropped to 446 in FY2004. The questions remain, however, whether field agents continue to be allocated to organized crime matters at similar rates to those before the terrorist attacks of September 11, 2001, and subsequent FBI reorganization, and whether these agents continue to be utilized at lower rates than which they are allocated [46]

This disparity between FBI field agent allocation and field agent utilization may suggest several things. For one, it may suggest that organized crime posed less of a threat to the United States in 2004 than it did in 2000. However, recent actions and testimony by former Attorney General Michael Mukasey suggest the opposite may be true. Former Attorney General Mukasey reconvened the Organized Crime Council in April 2008, for the first time in 15 years [47]. He stated that he did so because organized crime—both domestic and international—remains a significant threat. The sustained threat does not explain the decrease in field agent utilization in these matters.

A second possible reason for the disparity in field agent allocation and utilization is that although the FBI did not intend to decrease its agent utilization on organized crime matters, agents may have been diverted to higher-priority issues such as counterterrorism.

In fact, the Department of Justice, OIG, reported that the FBI confirmed underutilizing organized crime resources because the field divisions committed to prioritizing counterterrorism first and foremost. The FBI diverted agents from traditional crime squads—such as organized crime—and moved them to counterterrorism squads [48].

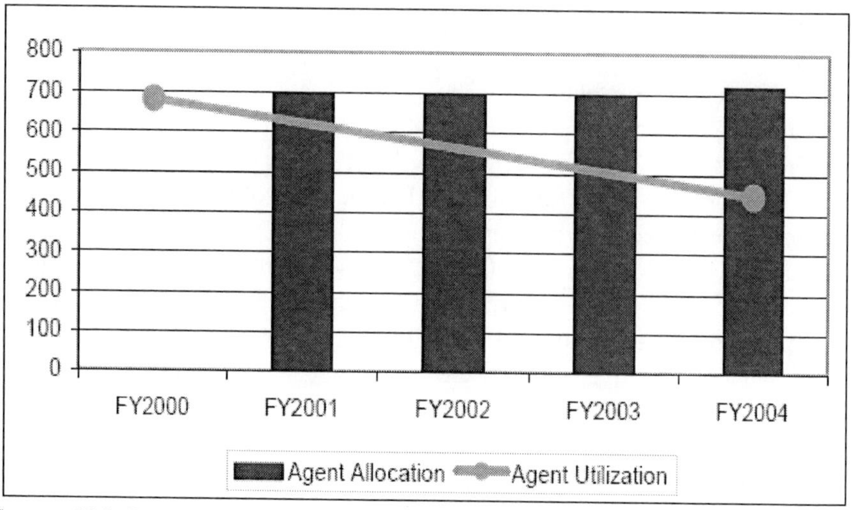

Source: U.S. Department of Justice, Office of the Inspector General, Audit Division, The External Effects of the Federal Bureau of Investigation's Reprioritization Efforts, Audit Report 05-37, September 2005, pp. 73-75, http://www.us doj.gov/oig/reports/FBI/a0537/final.pdf.

Notes: The data on organized crime agent allocation come from the OIG analysis of FBI Resource Management and Allocation (RMA) Office data. The data on organized crime agent utilization come from the OIG analysis of FBI Time Utilization Recordkeeping (TURK) data. The FBI utilized 35% fewer agents on organized crime matters in FY2004 than it did in FY2000. FBI organized crime agent allocation data were not available to the OIG for FY2000 because prior to FY2001, the FBI allocated organized crime and drug resources together.

Figure 1. FBI Allocation and Utilization of Agents on Organized Crime Matters, FY2000-FY2004.

A third potential explanation is that the FBI lacks the man-power and monetary resources to address all significant threats that the country faces. This lack of resources may act in conjunction with the FBI's prioritization of counterterrorism. FBI Director Robert Muller has stated that indeed resources have shifted away from traditional crime fighting, and that there is a need to restore the criminal programs to "appropriate resource levels" [49].

Case Openings

In FY2000, the FBI had 682 field agents investigating organized crime, and they initiated (opened) 433 organized crime investigations (cases) in that year, as shown in Table 1. Thus, the number of cases per agent was about 0.6. In FY2004, the FBI had 433 field agents investigating organized crime, and they initiated 263 organized crime investigations. Therefore, the number of cases per agent was also about 0.6.50 Taken alone, a decrease in the number of organized crime cases could suggest that the threat from organized crime is actually decreasing. However, the number of agents investigating organized crime decreased proportionally to the number of organized crime cases opened. Therefore, using data from the number of organized crime case openings does not alone provide a reliable indication of the organized crime threat. There are several possible explanations for the simultaneous decrease in agents investigating organized crime matters and the number of organized crime case openings. One possibility is that a reduction in organized crime activity—and thus a reduction in the number of organized crime cases opened—could lead to fewer agents needed to investigate organized crime matters. On the other hand, a reduction in agents working on organized crime cases could lead to a reduction in the overall number of these cases opened and may not actually reflect a decrease in organized crime activity. One possible side effect of a decrease in the number of federal agents investigating organized crime may be an increased workload for each agent working on these cases; if the organized crime threat is sustained—as has been suggested by DOJ officials—it is possible that the caseloads of organized crime agents could increase if the number of agents actually investigating organized crime is sustained or further decreased [51].

Table 1. FBI Organized Crime Cases Worked Per Agent, FY2000 and FY2004

Fiscal Year	Organized Crime Agent Utilization	Number of Organized Crime Cases Opened	Organized Crime Cases/Agent
2000	682	433	0.63
2004	446	263	0.59

Prosecutions

The Department of Justice, Organized Crime and Racketeering Section (OCRS), oversees federal organized crime prosecutions. As noted earlier, OCRS has organized crime Strike Force Units in 21 of the 94 U.S. Attorneys'

Offices (USAOs) where there exists a large organized crime presence in that district.

Figure 2 graphs the number of organized crime cases referred to the USAOs for prosecution from FY1999 through FY2008. As evidenced in the figure, there has not been a consistent increase or decrease in the number of organized crime cases filed with the USAOs across these years.

Many factors could influence the number of organized crime cases referred to the USAOs for prosecution. While this number could reflect the actual activities of organized crime groups, several factors suggest that the trends in prosecutions may not mirror the trends in organized criminal activity—either in type or in number.

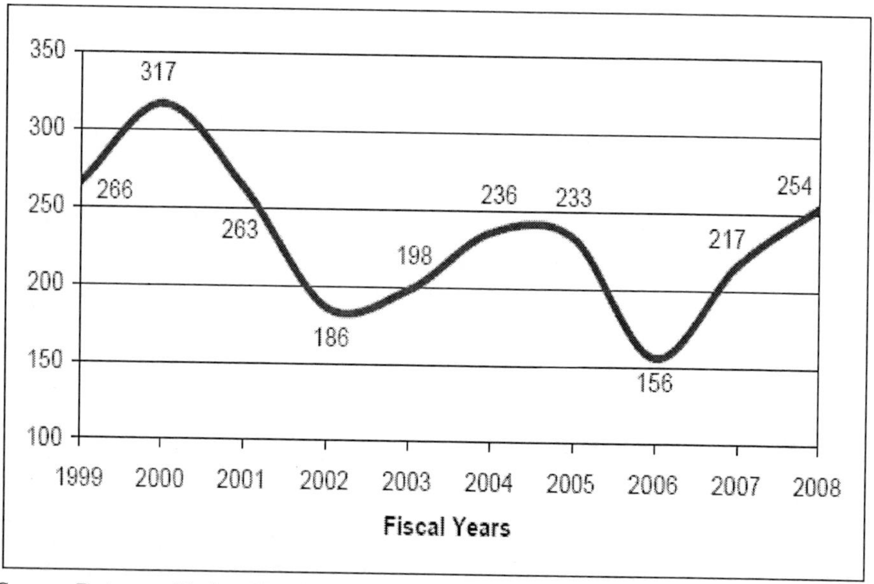

Source: Data provided to CRS by the USAO.

Notes: These data include organized crime cases filed with the USAOs from all federal agencies.

Figure 2. Organized Crime Cases Filed with the U.S. Attorneys' Offices, FY1999-FY2008.

Firstly, prosecutions may be driven in part by Administration priorities, which may not emphasize all federal crimes equally. Secondly, organized crime cases that are actually prosecuted are only a small subset (and not necessarily a proportionate subset) of those crimes committed [52]. Therefore, the number of organized crime prosecutions alone provides little evidence as to the true trends in organized criminal activity.

One question that remains is whether the resources and tools for investigating and prosecuting organized crime in the United States—as previously provided by Congress—are the most effective tools for combating today's threats from organized crime.

Current Organized Crime Trends

As mentioned, organized crime in the United States has taken on an increasingly transnational nature. This shift has been facilitated by factors such as economic globalization and improved communications technology [53]. The section below provides a detailed discussion of the organized crime groups that operate in the United States, the activities of these groups, and the domestic industries that have been and may continue to be threatened by organized crime.

One way of analyzing the organized crime threat is by examining the most prominent organized crime groups operating in the United States. The FBI, for instance, provides information on the various organized crime groups in order to present a picture of organized crime in the United States. A second method is by examining those areas of society threatened most by the activities of organized crime (such as the economy or national security), regardless of which group is committing the crime. The Organized Crime and Racketeering Section (OCRS) at DOJ, for example, presents the organized crime threats to the United States in terms of the principal threat areas, rather than the individual groups committing crimes. Subsequent discussion uses both approaches to analyze organized crime.

Organized Crime Groups Operating in the United States [54]

Although organized crime is popularly associated with the Italian Mafia, the breadth of organized crime in the United States includes many other criminal organizations. The FBI investigates organized crime groups that fall into three major categories: (1) La Cosa Nostra, Italian organized crime, and racketeering; (2) Eurasian/Middle Eastern organized crime; and (3) Asian and African criminal enterprises [55]. Figure 3 outlines the top organized crime threats to the United States, as identified by the FBI. Threats to the United

States posed by selected large-scale criminal organizations are discussed below.

Source: The FBI identifies and provides an overview of these various organized crime groups on its website at http://www.fbi.gov/hq/cid/orgcrime/ocshome.htm.

Figure 3. Organized Crime Threats in the United States (According to the FBI).

Eurasian/Russian

The discussion of Russian organized crime tends to reference not only Russian crime syndicates, but a variety of Eurasian crime groups as well [56]. These groups began emerging in the United States in the late 1970s and became even more prevalent following the collapse of the Soviet Union in 1991. They are now considered by the FBI to be the top organized crime threat to the United States [57]. The Russian organized crime groups that operate in the United States exhibit less of a traditional hierarchical structure than the Italian Cosa Nostra, and they form their networks based more on the skills needed for particular crimes [58]. In the United States, Russian organized criminals are involved in long-established organized crime activities such as extortion, abduction, human smuggling, prostitution, drug trafficking, and theft, as well as white-collar criminal activities including money laundering and fraud of various types. In fact, the FBI has indicated that roughly 60% of FBI cases targeting Russian organized crime involve fraud [59] The types of fraud and scams that Russian criminals participate in cross industries from health care and strategic commodities (e.g., precious metals) fraud to credit card, insurance, securities, and investment fraud. They are also involved in scams in domains such as tax evasion and energy price rigging.

Many Russian organized crime groups operate in New York, New Jersey, Boston, Philadelphia, Chicago, Los Angeles, San Francisco, and Miami, among other cities [60].

U.S. law enforcement has relied heavily on RICO, money laundering, and asset forfeiture statutes to prosecute Russian crime syndicates. They consider these pieces of legislation as significant for combating organized crime activities as well as the structure of the criminal organizations [61]. Principal efforts to control Russian organized crime groups include the establishment of both domestic and international task forces and working groups aimed at dismantling these crime syndicates. Domestically, the FBI has set up task forces in cities such as New York, New Jersey, Philadelphia, Chicago, San Francisco, Los Angeles, and Miami. Also, local police departments in major cities, including New York and Los Angeles, have set up Russian organized crime task forces [62]. In addition, the FBI is involved in international working groups concerned with Russian organized crime, including the Eurasian Organized Crime Working Group; the Central European Working Group at the International Law Enforcement Academy in Budapest, Hungary; and the Southern European Cooperative Initiative in Bucharest, Romania. The FBI is also involved in an international organized crime task force in Budapest, Hungary, aimed at combating Russian organized crime; currently, this is the only international task force aimed at combating organized crime in which the FBI is involved. The FBI has indicated that this international effort has been invaluable in developing international partnerships and intelligence, as well as expanding its international capabilities [63]

Asian

Asian organized crime groups have had a presence in the United States since at least the early 1900s. However, there has been an increase in Asian organized crime since the 1990s [64]. Research indicates that there is not one unified Asian organized crime group; rather, there exist numerous crime syndicates, some more traditionally organized than others [65] According to the FBI, traditional groups include Chinese triads from Hong Kong, Taiwan, and Macau, and the Japanese Yakuza. Less traditional groups include tongs, triads, and Asian street gangs such as the Big Circle and the Fuk Ching. Similar to a trend seen among Russian organized crime groups, an emerging trend seen among Asian crime syndicates is a willingness to cooperate across ethnic and racial lines if it is profitable for the enterprise. Asian organized crime groups derive most of their profits from trafficking in drugs—such as heroin—and people, but are also actively involved in other criminal activities, from money laundering, counterfeiting, and fraud to kidnapping and the theft of autos, software, and clothing. The FBI indicates that Boston, Chicago, Honolulu, Las Vegas, Los Angeles, New Orleans, New York, Newark, Philadelphia, Portland, San Francisco, Seattle, and Washington, D.C,. are examples of areas with a high prevalence of Asian organized crime.

U.S. law enforcement has relied heavily on RICO, money laundering, and asset forfeiture statutes to prosecute Asian crime syndicates. Similar to efforts aimed at combating Russian organized crime groups, U.S. law enforcement participates in domestic and international working groups aimed at combating Asian organized crime. Domestically, the Interagency Working Group on Alien Smuggling examines policy and investigative issues surrounding the smuggling of aliens and trafficking of women and children, including involvement of Asian organized crime groups in these activities. The FBI is also involved in international working groups concerned with Asian organized crime, including the FBI/National Police Agency of Japan Working Group, Interpol's Project Bridge, the International Asian Organized Crime Conference, the Canadian/United States Cross-Border Crime Forum, and the International Law Enforcement Academy in Bangkok, Thailand [66].

Italian

The La Cosa Nostra (LCN), is the most prominent Italian organized crime group operating in the United States [67]. Within the LCN, there are five principal crime families.6 8 The LCN is involved in an array of illegal activities, from gambling and loan sharking to drug trafficking and money laundering, that threaten American society [69]. Most members of the LCN operate in the New York metropolitan area, but there are also criminal operations in Boston, Chicago, Newark, Detroit, Philadelphia, and Miami [70] La Cosa Nostra has been operating in the United States since the 1920s and still poses a threat today.

Early congressional and law enforcement efforts to control organized crime were aimed directly at controlling the illegal activities of the Mafia (LCN). As discussed earlier, these early congressional efforts involved enacting the 1968 Omnibus Crime Control and Safe Streets Act (P.L. 90-351) and the 1970 Organized Crime Control Act and RICO (P.L. 91-452), as well as the asset forfeiture and money laundering statutes. Civil RICO lawsuits have been particularly effective in purging the LCN from legitimate industries and unions, such as the Las Vegas gaming industry, the New York moving and storage industries, and the union representing truckers servicing JFK airport in New York.71 In addition to federal RICO statutes, many states have also adopted RICO statues. Many believe that RICO has been the most powerful tool in combating La Cosa Nostra [72]. Despite these effective tools, the LCN remains a major organized crime threat to American society.

Balkan

The FBI identifies Balkan organized crime, and Albanian groups in particular, as among the most formidable organized crime groups today, as evidenced, in part, by an increase in Albanian-born individuals arrested in the United States [73]. Albanian organized crime groups emerged in the United States in the late 1980s and have evolved from being close knit families to allowing in outsiders with particular areas of criminal expertise. These groups are active in areas such as New York, Los Angeles, Las Vegas, Dallas, and Houston, to name a few. Balkan crime groups have been involved in various illegal activities such as gambling, extortion, robbery, counterfeit currency, drug trafficking, human smuggling, real estate fraud, money laundering, witness intimidation, and murder.

One emerging trend seen among Balkan organized crime groups is an increased cooperation with other organized crime groups—further evidence that Balkan organized crime is not just increasing, but expanding [74]. For example, the FBI has indicated that the LCN has partnered with Albanian organized crime in New York. There, the LCN is relying on the Albanians as their enforcers, and the Albanians have increasingly taken over some turf there that was previously dominated by the LCN.

Other Organized Crime Groups

The federal government recognizes threats from other organized crime groups that may not have the same notoriety as larger groups such as the LCN. For example, Middle Eastern Criminal Enterprises are primarily involved in organized theft, financial fraud, money laundering, and cigarette smuggling. Also, African crime syndicates—and particularly Nigerian groups—are involved in heroin trafficking, money laundering, and fraud (including insurance, bank, auto, healthcare, identity, and document fraud).

Of note, a trend among organized crime groups is that they begin by victimizing members of their own neighborhoods and ethnic communities, and then expand their illegal activities beyond these community lines. For example, in the 1920s Prohibition era, the Italian-American mafia began victimizing other Italians in the Five Points neighborhood of Little Italy in New York, before extending their activities to other neighborhoods of New York and the surrounding metropolitan area [75]. If this is indeed a common pattern across organized crime groups, then it is likely that emerging crime groups may expand their activities rather than restrict them to the areas in which they currently operate.

Domestic Impact of Organized Crime

The U.S. Department of Justice Organized Crime Council,76 chaired by the Deputy U.S. Attorney General, has identified eight strategic threats to the United States posed by international organized crime [77]. Of note, the term "international organized crime" includes not only those organized crime groups operating outside the borders of the United States, but within the U.S. borders as well. As mentioned earlier, the Council noted that international organized criminals have and may penetrate the energy and other strategic sectors of the economy; provide logistical and other support to terrorists, foreign intelligence services, and governments; smuggle/traffic people and contraband goods into the United States; exploit the United States and international financial system to move illicit funds; use cyberspace to target U.S. victims and infrastructure; manipulate securities exchanges and perpetrate sophisticated frauds; corrupt or seek to corrupt public officials in the United States and abroad; and use violence or the threat of violence as a basis for power.

Former U.S. Attorney General Michael Mukasey outlined strategic goals in combating these threats. These goals continue to include:

- targeting the largest organized crime threats,
- dismantling criminal organizations and removing their leadership,
- marshalling information from all available resources, and
- relying on all possible domestic and international tools and law enforcement partnerships [78]

One specific goal of the Organized Crime Council that may be of particular interest to Congress is to "provide law enforcement with updated legislation and operational procedures needed to combat international organized crime." [79] Specifically, the Organized Crime Council indicated that laws and regulations should be expanded, updated, or modified to afford the government the abilities to investigate and prosecute organized criminals that affect American society from outside U.S. borders. This suggests that federal law enforcement currently may not have the extraterritorial jurisdiction or the most effective tools to combat the evolving organized crime threats to the United States. The section below provides a detailed discussion of some potential impacts of organized crime, followed by possible issues that the 111th Congress may consider.

Impact of Organized Crime on the Economy

Considering the current economic downturn, some analysts may question the effect that organized crime may have on American society. Organized crime could further weaken the economy with illegal activities (such as cigarette trafficking and tax evasion scams) that result in a loss of tax revenue for state and federal governments. Their fraudulent activities in the domains of strategic commodities, credit, insurance, stocks, securities, and investments could further weaken the already-troubled financial and housing markets.

Money Laundering

Money laundering involves concealing the nature, location, source, ownership, or control of proceeds from an illegal activity or placing them back into further illegal activity [80]. The ill-gotten proceeds are laundered through a variety of methods to become "clean money." With the expansion of the Internet and increased globalization, the methods of money laundering continue to become increasingly complex and difficult to detect. The Financial Crimes Enforcement Network (FinCEN), under the Department of the Treasury, indicates that the routes for money laundering include banks, check cashers, money transmitters, businesses, and casinos. Money launderers use methods such as complex wire transfers, shell companies, and currency smuggling to hide their dirty money [81]

Money laundering became a federal crime in the Money Laundering Control Act of 1986 (P.L. 99-570). It came to Congress's attention that organized criminals were camouflaging their proceeds, and Congress strengthened the federal criminal statues to better combat criminal organizations [82]. Recently, the scope of the money laundering statute has come under examination. The statute prohibits financial transactions of proceeds from illicit activities, but it does not currently define what constitutes "proceeds." The Supreme Court ruled in United States v. Santos that in the money laundering statute, the term "proceeds" refers to profits rather than gross receipts [83].

Legislation has since been introduced in the 111th Congress to amend the money laundering statute. The Money Laundering Correction Act of 2009 (H.R. 1793) and the Money Laundering Control Enhancement Act of 2009 (S. 378) would clarify the statute so that the term "proceeds" includes gross receipts of an illegal activity. The Fraud Enforcement and Recovery Act of 2009 (S. 386) would clarify both the money laundering and international money laundering statutes. Namely, it would indicate that "proceeds" includes gross receipts of illegal activities. Also, it would extend the international money laundering statute to apply to tax evasion in addition to the crimes already included. Some experts have argued that expanding the predicate offenses for international money laundering could broaden the tools the federal government is able to rely upon when investigating and prosecuting organized crime that is increasingly crossing international lines.

Cigarette Trafficking

Law enforcement agencies have also noted that criminal syndicates' participation in the trafficking of contraband cigarettes poses a significant threat to American society. A number of different organized crime groups are involved in cigarette trafficking. This illicit activity indirectly threatens the American economy and American communities. Cigarette smuggling leads to lost tax revenue. Businesses, in turn, compensate by raising taxes for the consumer, ultimately placing the increased economic burden on the consumer [84]. Excessive economic burdens on the consumer are of particular concern now because of the current economic recession. Consequently, revenues that would assist in funding government programs are being illegally redistributed because of organized crime activities.

Piracy and Counterfeiting

There is evidence that organized criminals are becoming increasingly involved in the production and distribution of counterfeit and pirated goods [85]. In Los Angeles County alone, Russian, Asian, Eurasian, and Lebanese organized crime groups are among those that have been involved in intellectual property rights crimes.86 Industries targeted are broad, including the music and motion picture industries, clothing companies, luxury goods manufacturers, and the tobacco industry. The federal government has taken several steps so far in fighting these crimes. In fact, in March 2004, the Department of Justice created an Intellectual Property Task Force to combat the increase in intellectual property piracy and counterfeiting by organized crime groups. Also, the Office of the United States Trade Representative (USTR) has indicated that an Anti-Counterfeiting Trade Agreement (ACTA) is being formulated with other countries, including Australia, Canada, EU, Japan, Jordan, Korea, Mexico, Morocco, New Zealand, Singapore, Switzerland, and the United Arab Emirates. According to the USTR, one benefit of the ACTA is that it will help combat the piracy and counterfeiting that is an "easy source of revenue for organized crime" [87].

Counterfeit currency is another example of a domain in which many organized crime groups are involved. Asian organized crime groups in Los Angeles and New Jersey have been linked to the production of "supernotes," or fake $50 and $100 bills. This can not only lead to a loss in actual money (for those paid in the counterfeit currency), but it can damage the value of the U.S. dollar.88 Some experts and policy analysts have suggested that one possible legislative option to help counter the involvement of organized crime in piracy and counterfeiting may be to expand the organized crime and money laundering statutes to include large-scale piracy and counterfeiting tied to other criminal activities [89].

Organized Crime and Terrorists

In addition to concern surrounding the many industries in which organized criminals operate, both analysts and policymakers have expressed concern about the potential nexus between organized crime and terrorism. The principal distinction authorities make between organized crime groups and terrorist groups is motivation. Money motivates organized crime, and ideology motivates terrorism. Because of this fundamental difference, the National Intelligence Council expects that between now and 2020:

> [T]he relationship between terrorists and organized criminals will remain primarily a matter of business, i.e., that terrorists will turn to criminals who can provide forged documents, smuggled weapons, or clandestine travel assistance when the terrorists cannot procure these goods and services on their own. Organized criminal groups, however, are unlikely to form long-term strategic alliances with terrorists. Organized crime is motivated by the desire to make money and tends to regard any activity beyond that required to effect profit as bad for business. For their part, terrorist leaders are concerned that ties to non-ideological partners will increase the chance of successful police penetration or that profits will seduce the faithful [90]

Despite the difference in motivation for organized crime and terrorism, the linking element for the two is money. Terrorist organizations may obtain funding from criminal acts, similar to organized crime groups. Also, terrorist organizations may launder these funds, similar to criminal organizations [91]. One example of a domain in which both organized criminals and terrorists may both benefit monetarily is piracy. Although there is currently less evidence of terrorist involvement in piracy, this business is a high-profit, low-risk activity, attractive to both criminals and terrorists [92].

Even if organized crime groups and terrorist organizations do not form long-term alliances, the possibility of short-term business alliances may be of concern to citizens and policymakers alike. The FBI indicates that although it has not yet had a case of organized crime groups working directly with terrorists, the possibility exists, and it continue to be watchful for this nexus. Because organized criminals are monetarily motivated, the FBI believes that these criminals would be inclined to work with terrorists if offered sufficient funds [93]

Although there are few reported instances of organized crime groups actually aiding terrorists, there are reported instances of international organized criminals conspiring to provide support to terrorist organizations. One such instance is Viktor Bout, an international arms trafficker who has been charged with conspiring to sell weapons to the Revolutionary Armed Forces of Columbia (FARC) [94]. As mentioned earlier in this report, federal law enforcement distinguishes between organized crime groups and drug trafficking organizations. Although there are no reported instances of organized crime groups directly working with terrorists, there are reported instances of "narco-terrorism," or terrorism funded through the proceeds of drug trafficking; the Liberation Tigers of Tamil Eelam, members of Hizbollah, and the Al-Qaida network are all examples of terrorist groups with close ties to drug trafficking [95]. GAO reports that U.S. officials are concerned with the threat in Eurasia of the links between terrorist organizations and organized crime, and trafficking in persons and drugs.96 With the prevalence of drug trafficking in the United States (via drug trafficking organizations as well as via organized crime groups that also have a hand in drug trafficking), policymakers may question (1) to what extent there is a nexus between domestic organized crime and terrorism and (2) what measures will most effectively combat both terrorism and organized crime.

POTENTIAL ISSUES FOR CONGRESS

The evolving nature of organized crime, as discussed, presents several issues that Congress may wish to consider. One issue is whether the tools that Congress has provided the federal government with to investigate and prosecute domestic organized crime—namely RICO, money laundering, and asset forfeiture statutes—are still effective tools to combat today's threats from organized crime. As evidenced by proposed legislation, Congress is considering clarifying and expanding these statutes so as to better equip the federal government to fight organized crime.

Federal Organized Crime Resources

Policies exist that allow federal law enforcement to investigate and prosecute organized crime groups. What may not fully exist, however, are the monetary and personnel resources to effectively combat organized crime—evidenced by a decrease in FBI agents used to investigate organized crime matters and in FBI organized crime case openings.

As previously discussed, in FY2004, the FBI utilized about 35% fewer agents on organized crime matters than it did in FY2000. The FBI has recognized that prioritizing counterterrorism and counterintelligence cases affects resources available to criminal investigations and that targeting the most significant threats will allow criminal investigative resources to be used most effectively. FBI Director Robert Muller testified to the need for restoring resources to the FBI's criminal programs, which include organized crime [97] Efforts—both administrative and congressional—can be made to this effect in several ways. One congressional option may be to increase overall funding available to the FBI and other federal law enforcement agencies that may be experiencing a decrease in resources dedicated to more traditional crime fighting matters, including organized crime. If these resources are then administratively allocated to criminal programs, organized crime agent utilization could potentially be more closely aligned with agent allocation without taking resources away from higher priority areas. Another congressional option may be to provide directed funding for organized crime matters. This option could ensure that any increase in funding intended to be directed toward criminal programs or organized crime matters would be utilized in those domains.

Yet another policy option may be to decide that the existing resources dedicated to organized crime are sufficient, given the limited financial resources available under the federal budget and given the national priority of combating the threats from terrorism. If, on the other hand, more funding were available or if the link between organized crime and terrorism were more direct, the case for reevaluating the funding directed toward organized crime might be stronger. However, considering the current budget constraints and priorities, some may consider existing organized crime funding as adequate.

Multilateral Crime Fighting

The federal government is already involved in several multilateral efforts—with state and local agencies as well as with international allies—to combat organized crime. With respect to working with domestic state and local law enforcement agencies, federal law enforcement agencies have formed joint task forces, some that target a variety of organized crime groups and some that target specific criminal organizations. Several of these task forces were outlined in previous sections of this report. Some analysts have suggested that despite the benefits of multilateral crime fighting, potential jurisdictional issues may arise. As organized crime groups have expanded their activities beyond state and even national lines, so has the responsibility for combating organized crime expanded. There exists a clear line between state and federal jurisdiction for prosecuting crimes. However, jurisdiction over agency responsibility for investigating cases may at times be unclear. This may be due in part to overlapping agency responsibilities and may also arise from the complexity of the cases investigated. For instance, an organized crime case with a drug component may fall under the jurisdiction of both the FBI and the DEA, potentially causing confusion on which agency would take the lead on such cases.

An issue that may become more visible than the issue of domestic law enforcement coordination is that of international law enforcement coordination. By ratifying the United Nations Convention Against Transnational Organized Crime in 2005, Congress took a step in working with foreign governments and law enforcement agencies to combat organized crime. Specifically, this Convention provided the framework for international cooperation by requiring mutual legal assistance between countries in fighting organized crime, as well as by requiring extradition for those organized criminal offenses outlined in the Convention. These provisions enhance the United States' ability to combat international organized crime and work with countries where there was no previous mutual assistance arrangement already in place [98].

As organized crime becomes increasingly transnational, so may the need for international organized crime working groups, task forces, and law enforcement cooperation. The benefits of international cooperation and partnerships are twofold. U.S. law enforcement can extend its expertise and capabilities to assist overseas law enforcement combat organized crime. Partnering with international law enforcement will develop the intelligence needed to support domestic investigations of organized crime [99]. However, one of the challenges, as expressed by federal law enforcement, is the increased time required to conduct international investigations [100]. Among the various effects that this may have on investigations, organized crime groups may be inadvertently afforded a longer time to conduct their illegal activities, potentially affecting a greater number of victims or increasing the magnitude of damage to the victims. A second challenge relating to international investigations may arise from the domestic practice that federal prosecutors are involved at all stages of organized crime cases. When investigations are conducted abroad, the involvement of prosecutors may not be as consistent.

In addition to law enforcement collaboration with foreign nations, Congress has given the federal government extraterritorial jurisdiction to investigate and prosecute individuals who criminally violate U.S. interests abroad (P.L. 99-399) [101]. This legislation was directed at combating terrorist acts against the United States, and thus the extraterritorial jurisdiction does not necessarily cover all crimes committed by organized crime groups. The increasingly transnational nature of organized crime as well as the potential for a nexus between organized crime and terrorism—as suggested by some analysts—may lead policymakers to question whether and/or how to extend this extraterritorial jurisdiction beyond the crimes currently covered with the practical and diplomatic challenges that such an approach may entail.

Potential Organized Crime Nexus with Terrorism

Some experts have indicated that the lines between organized crime groups and terrorist organizations may become increasingly blurry [102]. Even if organized crime groups and terrorist organizations do not form "long-term strategic alliances," as suggested by the National Security Council, [103] the links between organized crime and terrorism may still be significant. The Council suggests (as does the FBI), however, that organized criminals and terrorists may ally for business purposes. Both criminal and terrorist organizations depend on money; organized criminals are profit-driven, and terrorists—though ideology-driven—need money and goods to finance their operations. It has been suggested that organized crime groups may cooperate with terrorists if the business alliance is profitable.

Some experts have cited potential additional areas of overlap between organized crime groups and terrorist organizations. For example, the language school that provided some visas for the 9/11 hijackers is also reported to have provided visas for prostitutes of a human trafficking ring [104]. There have also been instances of terrorist organizations drawing on the structure and activities of organized crime groups as models for structuring their organizations and financing their operations. Drug trafficking, for instance, has been one of the most profitable activities for both organized crime groups and terrorist organizations. Other illegal activities include human trafficking, weapons trafficking, endangered species trafficking, art and antique theft, counterfeiting, and credit card fraud [105].

Because there may be overlap between organized crime groups and terrorist organizations in terms of their criminal activities and funding sources, some analysts have argued that combating organized crime is central to combating terrorism [106]. Congress therefore may consider the potential nexus between organized crime and terrorism when addressing the nation's security and determining the appropriate allocation and utilization of resources, as well as effective information sharing and interagency cooperation, as discussed above.

LEGISLATION IN THE 111TH CONGRESS

The Public Corruption Prosecution Improvements Act (S. 49), as introduced in the Senate, would among other things, expand the RICO statute by expanding the list of predicate offenses for racketeering. In particular, provisions of this Act would include "embezzlement or theft of public money, property, or records" as well as "theft or bribery concerning programs receiving Federal funds" in the list of RICO predicate offenses. Further, this Act would authorize evidence of these two crimes as a legal basis for the FBI or other investigative agency with jurisdiction to institute a wiretap. Although this bill is intended to combat public corruption in general, it would also expand the federal government's ability to investigate and prosecute organized crime and would extend to instances where public officials may be corrupted by organized crime.

Several bills in the 111th Congress are directly aimed at combating money laundering. As mentioned before, in United States v. Santos, the U.S. Supreme Court ruled that in the money laundering statute, the term "proceeds" refers to profits rather than gross receipts [107] Two bills in the 111th Congress would amend this statute. The Money Laundering Correction Act of 2009 (H.R. 1793), as introduced in the House; the Money Laundering Control Enhancement Act of 2009 (S. 378), as introduced in the Senate; and the Fraud Enforcement and Recovery Act of 2009 (S. 386), as favorably reported by the Senate Committee on the Judiciary, would all amend the money laundering statute so that the term "proceeds" includes gross receipts of an illegal activity.

S. 386 would also extend the international money laundering statute to apply to tax evasion (via moving money outside of the United States) in addition to the crimes already included.

REFERENCES

[1] U.S. Department of Justice, "Remarks prepared for delivery by Attorney General Michael B. Mukasey on International Organized Crime at the Center for Strategic and International Studies," press release, April 23, 2008, http://www.usdoj.gov/ag/speeches/2008/ag-speech-080425.html.

[2] Ibid. The Organized Crime Council began meeting in 1970 and continued through 1993. When former Attorney General Michael Mukasey reconvened the Council in 2008, this was the first time it had met in 15 years.

[3] Department of Justice, Office of the Inspector General, Audit Division, *The External Effects of the Federal Bureau of Investigation's Reprioritization Efforts*, Audit Report 05-37, September 2005, p. 73. This statement is based on statistics from the FBI alone, not including other federal law enforcement agencies. The FBI is the federal law enforcement agency most involved in investigating organized crime matters.

[4] James O. Finckenauer, "Problems of Definition: What is Organized Crime?" *Trends in Organized Crime*, vol. 8, no. 3 (Spring 2005), pp. 63-82.

[5] According to the FBI, there are four main Italian organized crime groups operating in the United States: the Sicilian Mafia (from which the LCN was formed), the Camorra or Neapolitan Mafia, the 'Ndrangheta or Calabrian Mafia, and the Sacra Corona Unita or United Sacred Crown. The term "Mafia" tends to be an encapsulating term referencing all of these groups.

[6] Federal law enforcement tends to refer to organized crime groups as distinct from drug trafficking organizations (DTOs) or gangs. Therefore, this report does not include specific discussions of DTOs or gangs. For more information on DTOs (Mexican DTOs, in particular), see the archived CRS Report RL34215, Mexico's Drug Cartels, by Colleen W. Cook. For more information on gangs, see CRS Report RL341 12, *Gangs in Central America*, by Clare Ribando Seelke; CRS Report RL34233, *The MS-13 and 18th Street Gangs: Emerging Transnational Gang Threats?* by Celinda Franco; and archived CRS Report RL33400, *Youth Gangs: Background, Legislation, and Issues*, by Celinda Franco.

[7] RICO is codified at 18 U.S.C. § 1961-1968.

[8] As defined in 18 U.S.C. § 1961, an "'enterprise' includes any individual, partnership, corporation, association, or other legal entity, and any union or group of individuals associated ... although not [necessarily] a legal entity," and a "'pattern of racketeering activity' requires at least two acts of racketeering activity" to occur within 10 years of one another for a criminal organization to be prosecuted for racketeering. Racketeering is defined as any number of violations, including an act or threat involving murder, kidnapping, gambling, arson, robbery, bribery, extortion, or dealing in a controlled substance. See 18 U.S.C. § 1961 for a comprehensive list of the predicate offenses for racketeering.

[9] Frank Browning and John Gerassi, *The American Way of Crime* (New York: G.P. Putnam and Sons, 1980), p. 53.

[10] U.S. Congress, House Government Operations, Legal and Monetary Affairs, *Federal Effort Against Organized Crime: Report of Agency Operations*, committee print, 90th Cong., 2nd sess., June 1968.

[11] Congressional testimony in 1963 by Joseph Valachi—a prominent member of the LCN Genovese crime family— shed light on the true extent of the LCN network. Joseph Valachi was the first Mafia member to publicly affirm the existence of a criminal organization such as the LCN. In 1963, he testified before the Permanent Subcommittee on Investigations of the Senate Committee on Government Operations. For text of his complete testimony, please see U.S. Congress, Senate Committee on Government Operations, Permanent Subcommittee on Investigations, *Organized Crime and Illicit Traffic in Narcotics*, 88th Cong., 1st sess., September 25, 1963.

[12] Task Force on Organized Crime, *Task Force Report: Organized Crime: Annotations and Consultants' Papers*, The President's Commission on Law Enforcement and Administration of Justice, Washington, 1967, p. 14.

[13] From remarks by Rep. Dante B. Fascell, Chairman, in U.S. Congress, House Committee on Government Operations, Subcommittee on Legal and Monetary Affairs, *The Federal Effort Against Organized Crime. Part 1*, 90th Cong., 1st sess., April 5, 1967.

[14] From remarks by Fred M. Vinson, Jr., Assistant Attorney General, Criminal Division, Department of Justice, in U.S. Congress, House Committee on Government Operations, Subcommittee on Legal and Monetary Affairs, *The Federal Effort Against Organized Crime. Part 1*, 90th Cong., 1st sess., April 5, 1967.

[15] For this analysis, CRS used the data referenced in the U.S. Congress, House Committee on Government Operations, Subcommittee on Legal and Monetary Affairs, *The Federal Effort Against Organized Crime. Part 1*, 90th Cong., 1st sess., April 5, 1967. Convictions carry a greater burden of proof than indictments, and thus are more difficult for prosecutors to obtain. While the raw numbers of both indictments and convictions were on the rise, the proportion of indicted individuals who were later convicted decreased; this may suggest that organized crime was perhaps growing at a rate faster than the criminal justice system was able to handle.

[16] Task Force on Organized Crime, Organized *Crime: Report of the Task Force on Organized Crime*, National Advisory Committee on Criminal Justice Standards and Goals, Washington, 1976.

[17] U.S. Congress, Senate Committee on the Judiciary, *Organized Crime Control Act of 1969*, report to accompany S. 30, 91st Cong., 1st sess., December 16, 1969, S.Rept. 91-617.

[18] The LEAA administered federal funding for state and local law enforcement agencies, educational programs, research, and crime initiatives. It is no longer in existence and has since been succeeded by the Office of Justice Programs (OJP).

[19] The Omnibus Crime Control and Safe Streets Act was later amended by the Violent Crime Control and Law Enforcement Act of 1994. This amended Act addressed organized crime in that it expressed the sense of the Senate that "the United States should encourage the development of a United Nations Convention on Organized Crime." Five years later in 1999, the United Nations began developing a Convention against Transnational Organized Crime. The Omnibus Crime Control and Safe Streets Act was also amended by the Electronic Communications Privacy Act (ECPA) of 1986 (P.L. 99-508), which substantially revised Title III and related provisions. For more information on the ECPA, see CRS Report 98-326, *Privacy: An Overview of Federal Statutes Governing Wiretapping and Electronic Eavesdropping*, by Gina Stevens and Charles Doyle.

[20] Remarks from Sen. John L. McClellan, U.S. Congress, House Judiciary, No. 5, *Organized Crime Control*, 91st Cong., 2nd sess., May 20, 1970.

[21] Remarks from John N. Mitchell, Attorney General of the United States, U.S. Congress, House Judiciary, No. 5, *Organized Crime Control*, 91st Cong., 2nd sess., May 21, 1970.

[22] 18 U.S.C. § 3521. Although the foundation for the Witness Security Program was authorized by the Organized Crime Control Act of 1970, the program was established under Part F of Chapter XII of P.L. 98-473.

[23] RICO is codified at 18 U.S.C. § 1961-1968. For more information on RICO, please see CRS Report 96-950, *RICO: A Brief Sketch*, by Charles Doyle.

[24] See Howard Abadinsky, *Organized Crime*, 7th ed. (Belmont, CA: Wadsworth, 2003).

[25] See 18 U.S.C. § 1961 for a comprehensive list of the predicate offenses for racketeering. Offenses include—but are not limited to—crimes such as murder, kidnapping, gambling, arson, robbery, bribery, extortion,

dealing in obscene matter, dealing in a controlled substance or listed chemical, counterfeiting, theft from interstate shipment, embezzlement from pension and welfare funds, embezzlement from union funds, fraud and related activity in connection with identification documents or access devices, mail fraud, wire fraud, financial institution fraud, procurement of citizenship or nationalization unlawfully, obstruction of justice or criminal investigations, tampering with or retaliating against a witness, false statements or forgery in application and use of a passport or other documents, peonage, slavery, trafficking in persons, interference with commerce, and laundering of monetary instruments.

[26] Federal Bureau of Investigation, "Move Over, Mafia: The New Face of Organized Crime," press release, February 13, 2009, http://www.fbi.gov/page2/feb09/organizedcrime_021309.html.

[27] For more information on forfeiture, see CRS Report 97-139, Crime and Forfeiture, by Charles Doyle. Forfeiture comes in two forms: civil and criminal. Both result in the confiscation of property derived from or used in criminal activities. Criminal forfeiture is confiscation accomplished as part of the prosecution of the property owner. Civil forfeiture is accomplished through a civil proceeding ordinarily brought against the property involved in the illicit activity.

[28] Money laundering is codified at 18 U.S.C. § 1956. The Money Laundering Control Act is Subtitle H of Title I of the Anti-Drug Abuse Act of 1986. For more information on the federal money laundering statutes, see CRS Report RL33315, *Money Laundering: An Overview of 18 U.S.C. 1956 and Related Federal Criminal Law*, by Charles Doyle and Todd Garvey

[29] In addition to the legislative efforts to control organized crime, there have been other national efforts aimed at assessing the activities of organized crime in the United States and providing recommendations for curbing its impact on society. Examples of advisory groups tasked with assessing the status of organized crime include the National Advisory Committee on Criminal Justice Standards and Goals (Organized Crime Task Force of 1976), the President's Commission on Organized Crime that met from 1983 through 1986, and the Organized Crime Council that met from 1970 to 1993. These groups have consistently concluded that organized crime remains a significant threat.

[30] Carrie Johnson, "Obama Team Faces Major Task in Justice Dept. Overhaul; Goal is to Restore Confidence in Law Enforcement Actions," *The Washington Post*, November 13, 2008, p. A02, Suburban Edition.

[31] U.S. Department of Justice, "Remarks prepared for delivery by Attorney General Michael B. Mukasey on International Organized Crime at the Center for Strategic and International Studies," press release, April 23, 2008, http://www.usdoj.gov/ag/speeches/2008/ag-speech-080425.html.

[32] See the Department of Justice, Organized Crime and Racketeering Section website at http://www.usdoj.gov/criminal/links/ocrs.html.

[33] Because the FBI is the federal law enforcement agency leading the fight against organized crime, much of the discussion on federal crime control efforts in this report refers to the FBI. The examples used in this report, therefore, do not provide a comprehensive view of the federal efforts against organized crime.

[34] The FBI identifies organized crime threats on its website at http://www.fbi.gov/hq/cid/orgcrime/aboutocs.htm.

[35] From remarks by Chris Swecker, Acting Executive Assistant Director Law Enforcement Services, Federal Bureau of Investigation in U.S. Congress, House Committee on Homeland Security, Subcommittee on Management, Integration, and Oversight, *9/11 Reform Act: Examining the Implementation of the Human Smuggling and Trafficking Center*, 109th Cong., 2nd sess., March 8, 2006.

[36] While task forces tend to focus on investigating crimes, working groups tend to focus on discussing various threats and developing strategies to counter the threats.

[37] See the Federal Bureau of Investigation, Minneapolis Division Field Office website at http://minneapolis.fbi.gov/taskforces.htm#organized_crime.

[38] An example of one such task force is referenced in: Federal Bureau of Investigation, "Pedro D. Ruiz Named SAC of New York Field Office's Intelligence Division," press release, September 19, 2007, http://www.fbi.gov/pressrel/pressrel07/ruiz091707.htm.

[39] See the Department of Justice, Organized Crime and Racketeering Section website at http://www.usdoj.gov/criminal/links/ocrs.html.

[40] United Nations Office of Drugs and Crime, *United Nations Convention Against Transnational Organized Crime and the Protocols Thereto*, United Nations, New York, 2004.

[41] INTERPOL is the largest international police organization, composed of 187 member countries. It facilitates international law enforcement cooperation, primarily through maintaining secure global police communication systems, operating data services and databases for police, providing operational police support, and promoting police

training and development. For more information on INTERPOL, see http://www.interpol.int/.

[42] The USNCB transmits, responds to, and executes requests for international law enforcement cooperation in which the United States is involved. For more information on the USNCB, see http://www.usdoj.gov/usncb/.

[43] From remarks by Grant D. Ashley, Assistant Director, Criminal Investigative Division, Federal Bureau of Investigation, in U.S. Congress, Senate Committee on Foreign Relations, *Combating Transnational Crime and Corruption in Europe*, 108th Cong., 1st sess., October 30, 2003.

[44] Department of Justice, Office of the Inspector General, Audit Division, *The External Effects of the Federal Bureau of Investigation's Reprio ritization Efforts*, Audit Report 05-37, September 2005, p. 73.

[45] Ibid., p. 14.

[46] The specific number of agents allocated to and actually utilized on organized crime cases is not publically available after FY2004. For this reason, CRS is unable to determine the current relationship between agents allocated to and agents utilized on organized crime matters.

[47] U.S. Department of Justice, "Remarks prepared for delivery by Attorney General Michael B. Mukasey on International Organized Crime at the Center for Strategic and International Studies," press release, April 23, 2008, http://www.usdoj.gov/ag/speeches/2008/ag-speech-080425.html.

[48] Department of Justice, Office of the Inspector General, Audit Division, *The External Effects of the Federal Bureau of Investigation's Repr ioritization Efforts*, Audit Report 05-37, September 2005, pp. 74-75.

[49] From remarks by Robert S. Mueller III, Director, Federal Bureau of Investigation, in U.S. Congress, Senate Committee on Appropriations, *Commerce, Justice, Science, and Related Appropriations for FY2008*, 110th Cong., 1st sess., April 26, 2007, p. 305.

[50] U.S. Department of Justice, Office of the Inspector General, Audit Division, *The External Effects of the Federal Bureau of Investigation's Reprioritization Efforts*, Audit Report 05-37, September 2005, pp. 73-75, http://www.usdoj.gov/oig/reports/FBI/a0537/final.pdf. CRS calculated the number of cases per agent based on the number of agents reported to be working on organized crime matters and the number of organized crime cases reportedly opened for FY2000 and FY2004/

[51] The specific number of agents working on organized crime cases is not publically available after FY2004. For this reason, CRS is unable to

determine whether the workload of agents working organized crime cases has fluctuated from the FY2004 level.

[52] See the Bureau of Justice Statistics flowchart illustrating case flow through the criminal justice system at http://www.ojp.usdoj.gov/bjs/largechart.htm.

[53] Committee on Law and Justice, National Research Council, *Transnational Organized Crime: Summary of a Workshop*, ed. Peter Reuter and Carol Petrie (Washington: National Academy Press, 1999), pp. 1-2.

[54] As mentioned, drug trafficking organizations (DTOs) are considered by DOJ and the FBI as separate from organized crime groups. Although many organized crime groups are involved in drug smuggling, trafficking, and distribution— among various other crimes—DTOs' primary involvement is drugs. For more information on the U.S. policy and efforts to combat drug trafficking, see CRS Report RL32352, *War on Drugs: Reauthorization and Oversight of the Office of National Drug Control Policy*, by Mark Eddy.

[55] The FBI identifies organized crime threats on its website at http://www.fbi.gov/hq/cid/orgcrime/aboutocs.htm.

[56] For purposes of this discussion, the term Russian organized crime refers to both Russian and Eurasian crime groups operating in the United States. The FBI and other experts also reference the combination of Russian and Eurasian crime groups under an umbrella term. See, for example, James O. Finckenauer and Jay Albanese, "Organized Crime in North America," in *Handbook of Transnational Crime and Justice*, ed. Philip Reichel (Thousand Oaks, CA: Sage, 2005), pp. 439-456.).

[57] U.S. Congress, House Committee on International Relations, *Threat from International Organized Crime and Global Terrorism*, 105th Cong., 1st sess., October 1, 1997.

[58] Russian crime groups in Russia have a more hierarchical structure than those groups operating in the United States. These groups, such as the Vory V Zakone, or "thieves-in-law," exhibit a structure more similar to the Italian Cosa Nostra. See Alexander Sukharenko, "The Use of Corruption by 'Russian' Organized Crime in the United States," *Trends in Organized Crime*, vol. 8, no. 2 (Winter 2004), pp. 118-129. Also see James O. Finckenauer and Jay Albanese, "Organized Crime in North America," in *Handbook of Transnational Crime and Justice*, ed. Philip Reichel (Thousand Oaks, CA: Sage, 2005), pp. 439-456.

[59] From remarks by Grant D. Ashley, Assistant Director, Criminal Investigative Division, Federal Bureau of Investigation, in U.S. Congress, Senate Committee on Foreign Relations, *Combating Transnational Crime and Corruption in Europe*, 108th Cong., 1st sess., October 30, 2003.

[60] These are the cities in which the FBI has set up special investigative units dedicated to investigating Russian organized crime.

[61] Federal Bureau of Investigation, "Inside the FBI: Organized Crime," press release, February 13, 2009, http://www.fbi.gov/inside/archive/inside021309.htm.

[62] James O. Finckenauer and Jay Albanese, "Organized Crime in North America," in *Handbook of Transnational Crime and Justice*, ed. Philip Reichel (Thousand Oaks, CA: Sage, 2005), pp. 439-456

[63] Federal Bureau of Investigation, "Testimony of Grant D. Ashley, Assistant Director, Criminal Investigative Division, FBI Before the Subcommittee on European Affairs, Committee on Foreign Relations, United States Senate," press release, October 30, 2003, http://www.fbi.gov/congress/congress03/ashley103003.htm.

[64] Glenn E. Curtis, Seth L. Elan, and Rexford A. Hudson, et al., "Transnational Activities of Chinese Crime Organizations: A Report Prepared under an Interagency Agreement by the Federal Research Division, Library of Congress," *Trends in Organized Crime*, vol. 7, no. 3 (Spring 2002), pp. 19-57.

[65] Ko-Lin Chin, *Chinatown Gangs: Extortion, Enterprise, Ethnicity* (New York: Oxford University Press, 2000).

[66] Federal Bureau of Investigation, Organized Crime: Asian Criminal Enterprises, http://www.fbi.gov/hq/cid/orgcrime/asiancrim.htm.

[67] According to the FBI, there are four main Italian organized crime groups operating in the United States: the Sicilian Mafia (from which the LCN was formed), the Camorra or Neapolitan Mafia, the 'Ndrangheta or Calabrian Mafia, and the Sacra Corona Unita or United Sacred Crown. The term "Mafia" tends to be an encapsulating term referencing all of these groups.

[68] The five principal crime families that make up the LCN are the Bonanno, the Colombo, the Genovese, the Gambino, and the Luchese families.

[69] Other principal threats that the LCN poses to American society are labor racketeering, political corruption, extortion, theft, bribery, kidnapping,

fraud, counterfeiting, infiltration of legitimate businesses, murders, and bombings.

[70] James O. Finckenauer, *La Cosa Nostra in the United States*, International Center, National Institute of Justice, 2007, http://www.docstoc.com/docs/416307/La-Cosa-Nostra-in-the-Unites-States---2000.

[71] Frank J. Marine, Organized Crime and Racketeering Section, United States Department of Justice, Washington, District of Columbia, USA, "The effects of organized crime on legitimate business," *Journal of Financial Crime*, vol. 13, no. 2 (2006), pp. 2 14-234.

[72] James B. Jacobs, Christopher Panarella, and Jay Worthington, *Busting the Mob: United States v. Cosa Nostra* (New York: New York University Press, 1994).

[73] John DiStasio, "International Organized Crime Center," *United States Attorneys' Bulletin*, vol. 51, no. 5 (September 2003), pp. 2-6.

[74] Clint Williamson, "Balkan Organized Crime: The Emerging Threat," *United States Attorneys' Bulletin*, vol. 51, no. 5 (September 2003), pp. 42-48.

[75] *World Encyclopedia of Organized Crime*, ed. Jay Robert Nash (Dallas: Zane Publishing, 1995).

[76] The Organized Crime Council includes leaders from nine federal law enforcement agencies: the Federal Bureau of Investigation; the U.S. Drug Enforcement Agency; the Bureau of Alcohol, Tobacco, Firearms and Explosives; the U.S. Immigration and Customs Enforcement; the U.S. Secret Service; the Internal Revenue Service; the U.S. Postal Inspection Service; Diplomatic Security; and the U.S. Department of Labor, Office of the Inspector General.

[77] Organized Crime Council, *Overview of the Law Enforcement Strategy to Combat International Organized Crime*, U.S. Department of Justice, April 2008. In this Strategy, the Organized Crime Council uses the broad term international organized crime to include organized crime in the United States. Former U.S. Attorney General Michael Mukasey has underscored the inclusion of domestic organized crime under the umbrella term of international organized crime, citing the globalization of crime and of groups with member around the world (including the United States). See U.S. Department of Justice, "Remarks Prepared for Delivery by Attorney General Michael B. Mukasey on International Organized Crime at the Center for Strategic and International Studies," April 23, 2008, http://www.usdoj.gov/ag/speeches/2008/ag_speech_080423.html.

[78] U.S. Department of Justice, "Remarks Prepared for Delivery by Attorney General Michael B. Mukasey on International Organized Crime at the Center for Strategic and International Studies," April 23, 2008, http://www.usdoj.gov/ag/speeches/2008/ag_speech_080423.html.

[79] Organized Crime Council, *Overview of the Law Enforcement Strategy to Combat International Organized Crime*, U.S. Department of Justice, April 2008, pp. 14-15

[80] Money laundering is codified as a federal crime at 18 U.S.C. § 1956.

[81] See the Overview of Law Enforcement on the FinCEN website at http://www.fincen.gov/law_enforcement/.

[82] For more information on the money laundering discussions in Congress preceding the Money Laundering Control Act of 1986, see U.S. Congress, Senate Committee on the Judiciary, *Money Laundering Legislation*, Hearing on S. 572, S. 1335, and S. 1385, 99th Cong., 1st sess., October 29, 1985, S.Hrg. 99-540.

[83] "Supreme Court Narrows Scope of Money-Laundering Statute," *Criminal Justice Newsletter*, July 2008, pp. 1-3.

[84] U.S. Congressman Bobby Scott, "Prevent All Cigarette Trafficking Act of 2008," press release, September 9, 2008, (continued...)(...continued) http://www.bobbyscott.
house.gov/index.php?option=com_contentandtask=viewandid=346andIt emid=89.

[85] U.S. Government Accountability Office, *Intellectual Property: U.S. Efforts have Contributed to Strengthened Laws, but Significant Enforcement Challenges Remain*, GAO-05-788T, June 14, 2005, http://www.gao.gov/new.items/d05788t.pdf. Counterfeit and pirated goods are those that are either fake copies or copies that have been reproduced without authorization.

[86] From remarks by John C. Stedman, Lieutenant, Sheriff's Department, County of Los Angeles, before the U.S. Congress, Senate Committee on Homeland Security and Government Affairs, *Counterfeit Goods: Easy Cash for Criminals and Terrorists*, 109th Cong., 1st sess., May 25, 2005, p. 8. Intellectual property rights (IPR) include copyrights, trademarks, trade secrets, and patents.

[87] Office of the United States Trade Representative, Anti-Counterfeiting Trade Agreement (ACTA), August 4, 2008, http://www. ustr.gov/assets/Document_Library/Fact_Sheets/2008/asset_upload_file7 60_15084.pdf?ht=.

[88] Todd Bullock, "Narcotics, Counterfeiting Help Fund North Korea, U.S. Says: Senate hearing discusses Pyongyang's criminal operations," America.gov, April 26, 2006, http://www.america.gov/st/washfile-english/2006/April/20060426135925tjkcollub0.8716699.html.

[89] Gregory F. Treverton, Carl Matthies, and Karla J. Cunningham, et al., Film Piracy, Organized Crime, and Terrorism, RAND Corporation, Safety and Justice Program and the Global Risk and Security Center, 2009, http://www.rand.org/pubs/monographs/2009/RAND_MG742.pdf.

[90] *Mapping the Global Structure*, National Intelligence Council, Report of the National Intelligence Council's 2020 Project, Based on consultations with nongovernmental experts around the world, Washington, D.C., December 2004, p. 96.

[91] Angela Veng Mei Leong, "Criminal Finance: Money Laundering and Terrorist Financing," in *The Disruption of International Organised Crime: An Analysis of Legal and Non-Legal Strategies* (Burlington, VT: Ashgate Publishing Company, 2007), pp. 29-67.

[92] Gregory F. Treverton, Carl Matthies, and Karla J. Cunningham, et al., *Film Piracy, Organized Crime, and Terrorism*, RAND Corporation, Safety and Justice Program and the Global Risk and Security Center, 2009, http://www.rand.org/pubs/monographs/2009/RAND_MG742.pdf.

[93] Pat Milton, "FBI Worries About an Osama-Sopranos Link," Associated Press, October 1, 2006, http://www.redorbit.com/news/general/ 676652 /fbi_worries_about_an_osamasopranos_link/index.html.

[94] Organized Crime Council, *Overview of the Law Enforcement Strategy to Combat International Organized Crime*, U.S. Department of Justice, April 2008, p. 3.

[95] Ibid.

[96] U.S. General Accounting Office, *Combating Terrorism: Interagency Framework and Agency Programs to Address the Overseas Threat*, GAO-03-165, May 2003, http://www.gao.gov/new.items/d03165.pdf.

[97] From remarks by Robert S. Mueller III, Director, Federal Bureau of Investigation, in U.S. Congress, Senate Committee on Appropriations, *Commerce, Justice, Science, and Related Appropriations for FY2008*, 110th Cong., 1st sess., April 26, 2007, p. 305.

[98] From remarks by Bruce Swartz, Deputy Assistant Attorney General, Criminal Division, U.S. Department of Justice, at U.S. Congress, Senate Committee on Foreign Relations, *Hearing on Law Enforcement Treaties: Treaty Doc. 107-18, Inter-American Convention Against Terrorism; Treaty Doc. 108-6, Protocol of Amendment to the*

International Convention on the Simplification and Harmonization of Customs Procedures; Treaty Doc. 108-11, Council of Europe Convention on Cybercrime; Treaty Doc. 108-16, U.N. Convention Against Transnational Organized Crime and Protocols on Trafficking in Persons and Smuggling of Migrants, 108th Cong., 2nd sess., June 17, 2004, pp. 29-37.

[99] Examples of international law enforcement partnerships can be found on the FBI's website at http://www.fbi.gov/hq/cid/orgcrime/ lcnindex.htm#pantheon, http://www.fbi.gov/hq/cid/orgcrime/ asiancrim .htm, and http://www.fbi.gov/page2/feb09/organizedcrime_ 0213 09.html.

[100] U.S . Department of Justice, *The Electronic Frontier: The Challenge of Unlawful Conduct Involving the Use of the Internet*, A Report of the President's Working Group on Unlawful Conduct on the Internet, March 2000, p. Appendix B, http://www.usdoj.gov/criminal/ cybercrime/append.htm#B.

[101] See the Omnibus Diplomatic Security and Antiterrorism act of 1968, Title XII of P.L. 99-399. For more detailed information regarding the United States extraterritorial jurisdiction as well as the specific crimes are included in this jurisdiction, see CRS Report 94-166, *Extraterritorial Application of American Criminal Law*, by Charles Doyle.

[102] Thomas M. Sanderson, "Transnational Terror and Organized Crime: Blurring the Lines," *SAIS Review*, vol. XXIV, no. 1 (Winter-Spring 2004), pp. 49-61.

[103] *Mapping the Global Structure*, National Intelligence Council, Report of the National Intelligence Council's 2020 Project, Based on consultations with nongovernmental experts around the world, Washington, D.C., December 2004, p. 96.

[104] Louise Shelley, "The Globalization of Crime and Terrorism," *Global Issues*, February 2006, pp. 42-45.

[105] Ibid.

[106] Ibid.

[107] "Supreme Court Narrows Scope of Money-Laundering Statute," *Criminal Justice Newsletter*, July 2008, pp. 1-3.

In: Organized Crime, Gangs and Trafficking ISBN: 978-1-61122-829-8
Editors: C. Webb and P. Dobrev

Chapter 2

LEADING ORGANIZED CRIME PROBLEMS

James O. Finckenauer and Ko-Lin Chin

One thing we have learned from our recent interviews and research in Asia is that it is very hard to generalize about the problem of organized crime there. For example, there is little consensus among law enforcement authorities as to what the leading organized crime problems in Asia are. Nevertheless, if we are to try to generalize, our impression is that local law enforcement authorities in Asia seem to be more focused on traditional organized crime activities such as extortion, gambling, prostitution, loan sharking, debt-collection, and violence than they are on transnational organized crime activities such as drug trafficking, human smuggling /trafficking, arms trafficking, and money laundering. Moreover, many Asian officials are concerned with the nexus between gangsters and politicians, and especially the penetration of organized crime figures into business and politics. In this section, we will first briefly discuss some of the most important organized crime problems in the eight research sites, according to the information we received from our interviews with local authorities. We will then examine the viewpoint of American officials in Asia, and close by adding our own assessment. By traditional organized crime groups we mean groups that have continuity across crimes and over time, that engage in multiple criminal enterprises, that employ violence and corruption, and that usually have hierarchical structures.

ASIAN AUTHORITIES' PERSPECTIVE

The survey assessment of criminal organizations adapted from the United Nations' Center for International Crime Prevention for use here defines an "organized crime group" as "a structured group of three or more persons existing for a period of time acting in concert with the aim of committing one or more serious crimes or offences…in order to obtain, directly or indirectly, a financial or other material benefit." It further defines the transnational dimension of organized crime by the fact that the crimes are committed either in more than one country, or in one country but with preparation, planning, direction or control in another country. Beyond this guide, respondents were asked how their respective "governments" officially defined organized crime. Within that framework, the following is a relatively brief, country by country summary of the major organized crime issues and problems in the countries we visited.

China

For Chinese authorities, the most serious organized crime problems are, in order of seriousness: drug distribution, gambling, prostitution, and violence (He 2002, 2003). The Chinese government is alarmed by the dramatic increase in the number of heroin addicts in China, and the authorities believe that local and foreign-based drug syndicates are responsible for importing heroin from the neighboring Golden Triangle and distributing it throughout China (Ma 1994, Luo and Liang 1999, Zhao and Ke 2003). Gambling and prostitution have returned to China with a vengeance after they were practically wiped out by the Chinese Communists after the takeover in 1949 (Tse 2003, Si 2004). As crime groups are becoming better armed and more violent, Chinese authorities are also concerned with violent acts committed by mobsters against rival gang members, ordinary citizens, business owners, and government authorities (Xiao 2002).

As for the future, according to Chen Xiao-cun of the Criminal Investigation Division, Ministry of Public Security: "Our main concerns are: (1) mafia-like criminal organizations will penetrate into the legitimate business sector; (2) gangsters will get involved in politics and run for public office; and (3) they will eventually hook up with foreign-based organized crime groups." In fact, there is evidence to suggest that many crime groups in China have monopolized certain wholesale businesses and that the majority of these groups are protected by local authorities known as baohusan, or "protecting umbrella." In general, official corruption is seen to be a large and growing problem in China. Chen, and others, stressed that organized crime is largely a regional or citywide phenomenon in China – rather than a national or transnational phenomenon. Given the pace of economic development in China, and the interest of external investors in this development, the involvement of criminal organizations has significant implications, including a potential chilling effect upon the nature of economic growth.

Even though tens of thousands of Chinese men and women are being smuggled abroad every year, and the arrival of large numbers of undocumented Chinese laborers or sex workers is a major concern in many countries (Smith 1997, Kwong 1997, Emerton 2001, Brazil 2004), Chinese authorities do not consider this to be a major problem or view it as an organized crime problem. Some Chinese officials would even say that this is not a Chinese problem because most snakeheads (human smugglers) are Chinese-Americans (Chin 1999). Local authorities recounted to us the many benefits of having a large number of their own people working abroad and sending money home. Indeed, we observed considerable new housing development outside Fuzhou, which development is being fueled by monies allegedly sent home by illegal workers in the United States.

Taiwan

In Taiwan, the number one organized crime problem is heijin, the penetration of mobsters into the legitimate business sector and the political arena (Chin 2003). Many influential gangsters in Taiwan are now chief executive officers of major business conglomerates, and they are heavily involved in the businesses of bid-rigging, waste disposal, construction, cable television networks, telecommunications, stock trading, and entertainment. Since the mid-1980s, many crime figures, to protect themselves from police crackdowns, ran for public office and it is estimated that today one-third of the elected deputies in Taiwan are current or former gangsters.

Besides heijin, Taiwanese authorities are also concerned with "traditional" organized crime activities such as gambling, prostitution, loan sharking, debt-collection, extortion, and gang violence. Kidnapping for ransom is also a major concern for the authorities in Taiwan because influential and wealthy figures are often targeted and, as a result, a large number of Taiwanese entrepreneurs have left Taiwan for a safe haven abroad. It should be noted that none of these activities of major concern are of a transnational nature.

A relatively recent and growing crime problem that is transnational in nature is the production and distribution of pirated CDs and DVDs. Each of the three major criminal gangs surveyed in Taiwan is said to be involved in this business.

Even though Taiwan is a destination country for heroin from the Golden Triangle and amphetamine from China, Taiwanese authorities are more concerned with the influx of sex workers (or potential sex workers) from China, who are smuggled into Taiwan by boats across the Taiwan Strait or through fraudulent marriages with Taiwanese citizens (Chang 2002). The police sex raid, in which we participated, was for purposes of determining whether there were any illegal Chinese women working in those particular sex clubs, which are not otherwise illegal. The detention facility we visited was detaining, for periods of upwards to nine months or more, over 1,000 mostly young Chinese women awaiting deportation back to mainland China. According to the Taiwanese law enforcement authorities we interviewed, they are frustrated in dealing with the human smuggling issue because Chinese authorities are not cooperative, and because judges in Taiwan are reluctant to apply the country's anti-organized crime laws to the human trafficking networks. The latter is said to be because the judges do not regard this as an organized crime problem.

As was the case in Mainland China, our sources in Taiwan reported that there were no connections between organized crime groups and terrorist groups in Taiwan, nor was there evidence of any alliances of organized crime with armed opposition groups.

Hong Kong

Hong Kong has a most unusual status in that part of the world. It was a British colony for over a hundred years, returning to Chinese control in 1997 (van Kemenade, 1997). It now has the status of being a special administrative region, meaning a degree of autonomy and self-governance – although that is constantly in contention with the mainland. Hong Kong has a long tradition of being home to the criminal organizations known as triads (Chu 2000). It also has a strong history of combating these triads, and of combating corruption – for which it has one of the most sophisticated and well-resourced operations in the world (Lo 1993). At the same time, Hong Kong is very much subject to the illicit movement of goods, services, and people to and from the mainland. As to any U.S. interest, the DEA representative in Hong Kong told us that some 18 million tons of cargo destined for the United States pass through the port of Hong Kong in a year. This clearly poses a security concern for the U.S.

According to the elite Organized Crime and Triad Bureau (OCTB), Hong Kong Police (HKP), some of the leading organized crime problems in Hong Kong are: vehicle crime and smuggling, human smuggling, cross-border organized crime involving China and Macau, money laundering, drug trafficking, debt-collection, and triad monopolies. The latter include the control by triad societies of private bus routes, fish markets, street markets, wholesale markets, entertainment centers, parking services, fake VCD sales, prostitution, illegal gambling, and extortion. With respect to the fake VCDs, each of the Wo Shing Wo, the San Yee On, and the 14K are said to be involved in the manufacture and street-level distribution of pirated VCDs and DVDs.

As a major transportation and financial center of Asia and a transit point in and out of China, Hong Kong has been a hub for transnational organized crime activities for the past thirty years.

Although there are triad organizations active in Hong Kong, the OCTB indicated that there is no international triad organization. The DEA representatives in Hong Kong said that drug trafficking there was also not that well organized at the wholesale level. Instead, there are mainly small groups of individual entrepreneurs, and the triads are mostly involved in organizing the retail drug business at the street level.

The assessment done for us on major criminal organizations in Hong Kong indicates "they are not interested in involving themselves in politics." The kinds of political/ideological missions associated with terrorism are said not to be the missions of the Hong Kong triads.

Macau

Like Hong Kong, Macau is also a special administrative region, being a former Portuguese colony. The impression of Macau is that it is a tourist mecca, dominated by gambling casinos, prostitution, and drugs. Indeed, according to Sio-chak Wong, Director of the Judiciary Police of Macau, the two major organized crime problems in Macau are gambling and illegal immigration/prostitution. Gambling is dominated by triad groups transplanted from Hong Kong, while illegal immigration/prostitution is controlled by crime groups formed by mainland Chinese. Recently, these Chinese crime groups began to be involved in fraud, money laundering, and the smuggling of stolen goods from Macau to China.

Because the Macau administration relies heavily on taxes from the gambling industry, and prostitution is considered to be an important component to its gambling industry, Macau authorities are reluctant to crack down on crime groups active in gambling and prostitution. As a result, organized crime groups maintain a strong presence in the gambling business in Macau; at the same time, the sex industry in Macau is booming because of the arrival of large numbers of sex workers from China.

Japan

In Japan, the most serious organized crime problems are almost always related to the notorious Japanese organized crime groups – the yakuza (Hill 2003, Kaplan and Dubro 2003). Japanese authorities are mostly concerned with the yakuza's involvement in gambling, prostitution, amphetamine trafficking, and the victimization of legitimate businesses. According to Chief Ikegami of the Anti-organized Crime Division, Ueno Police Department, Tokyo Metropolitan Police, Japanese officials are alarmed by the presence of a large number of legal and illegal immigrants from China (mostly Shanghainese, Fujianese, and Northeasterners) who are involved in organized crime activities and who are considered to be heavily armed and dangerous.

Because of its wealth and the spending power of Japanese businessmen, Japan has become a major destination country for sex workers from Thailand, the Philippines, Colombia, China, Korea, and several other countries (Human Rights Watch 2000, Santos 2002). According to the latest Trafficking in Persons report from the U.S. State Department, Japan is currently a Tier 2 Watch List country. That list includes "countries whose governments do not fully comply with the Act's minimum standards but are making significant efforts to bring themselves into compliance with those standards, and:

a. The absolute number of victims of severe forms of trafficking is very significant or is significantly increasing; or
b. There is a failure to provide evidence of increasing efforts to combat severe forms of trafficking in persons from the previous year; or
c. The determination that a country is making significant efforts to bring themselves into compliance with minimum standards was based on

commitments by the country to take additional future steps over the next year" (U.S. Department of State 2004:29).

In addition to women from abroad, Japan also has a large number of local Japanese women who are involved in the sex trade (Kaplan and Dubro 2003).

Even though Japanese authorities are convinced that yakuza members are heavily involved in the transportation and control of foreign sex workers, they told us that it is not their number one priority because they believe foreign sex workers are not being forced into their activities, nor is there pressure from the Japanese public to do something about it.

The Philippines

Because of political instability and corruption, the country's economy is in bad shape, which results in a large number of Filipino people having to go overseas to work. Many of them are women, and a significant percentage of these women who leave with an "entertainer visa" end up working in the sex industry abroad (Santos 2002). Although the Philippine government has recently passed an anti-trafficking law, few human traffickers have ever been prosecuted and punished (U.S. Department of State 2004). The Philippines is also a Tier 2 Watch List country, according to the State Department. The Filipino officials we interviewed are more concerned with high profile crimes such as drug trafficking, kidnapping for ransom, hijacking, bank robbery, prostitution, illegal gambling, and firearms smuggling rather than the problem of Filipino sex workers abroad.

The trafficking of amphetamine (called shabu in the Philippines) from China to the Philippines has also been a major concern for the Filipino authorities for a long time. Recently, according to our Filipino subjects, many shabu laboratories have been established in the Philippines, in part because of the greater effectiveness of tighter coastal patrols in stopping the drug flow from abroad. The authorities we interviewed also indicated that the drug business in the Philippines is controlled by predominantly Filipino-Chinese, or Chinese from China, Hong Kong, and Taiwan who are protected by local politicians.

A U.S. government official interviewed in Manila indicated that organized crime and terrorism in the Philippines are different entities. The terrorist groups there are said to be mostly isolated groups and not involved in such transnational crimes as human trafficking and drug smuggling. A Philippines official did indicate that some terrorist groups may be involved in kidnapping for ransom, but they do not play a major role in such kidnappings because they are not strong in Manila, where most of the wealthy Chinese who are potential victims live.

Thailand

Undoubtedly, the two leading organized crime groups in Thailand are the jao pho (godfather) (Phongpaichit Piriyarangsan 1994) and the United Wa State Army (Gelbard 1998, Takano 2002). Jao pho are mostly ethnic Chinese based in the provinces who have business interests in both legitimate and criminal activities. Moreover, they have groups of associates and followers, move closely with powerful bureaucrats, policemen and military figures, sit in positions in local administration, and play a key role in parliamentary elections. According to Thai authorities, there are jao pho groups in 39 of Thailand's 76 provinces. The United Wa State Army (or the Red Wa) is another major concern for the Thai government because this organization, located in the Burmese part of the Golden Triangle, is believed to be responsible for the manufacturing and trafficking of millions of methamphetamine tablets (called yaba or mad drug in Thailand) into Thailand for local consumption. While heroin produced by the Red Wa and other groups in the Golden Triangle continues to pass through Thailand, the Thai authorities are, as in the past, less concerned with this because the heroin market in Thailand itself is relatively small.

Thailand has a well-established sex industry; it is also a source, transit, and destination country for trafficked women (Asia Watch 1993, Brown 2000, Jeffrey 2002). Because the sex trade is vital to the country's enormous tourist industry, and Thai policemen are believed to be heavily bribed by sex establishment owners, the sex business is not considered to be an organized crime problem by the Thai authorities. Nor are Thai officials concerned with the presence of a large number of Burmese sex workers in Thailand or in the trafficking of Thai women to Japan and Europe for sex work. Thailand is also a Tier 2 Watch List country.

Table 1. Leading Organized Crime Problems in Asia

	China	Taiw.	HK	Macau	Japan	Philip.	Thai.	Camb.
Drug Trafficking								
Heroin	H	M	H	L	L	L	L	M
Amphetamine	M	M	L	L	H	H	L	L
Methamphetaine	L	L	L	L	L	L	H	M
Drug Manufacturing								
Heroin	L	L	L	L	L	L	L	L
Amphetamine	H	L	L	L	L	H	L	L
Methamphetaine	L	L	L	L	L	L	M	M
Trafficking in women/ children for the sex industry	L	H	M	L	L	L	L	L
Trafficking in human beings for the purpose of labor	L	L	L	L	L	L	L	L
Human smuggling	L	M	M	L	H	L	M	L
Kidnapping for ransom	M	H	M	M	L	H	L	L
Gambling	H	M	M	H	H	H	H	M
Prostitution	H	H	H	L	M	M	M	L
Political-criminal nexus (bribery, corruption, and mafia politics)	H	H	L	L	H	H	H	L
Penetration into legitimate businesses	H	H	H	H	H	H	H	M

H = High Priority, M = Medium Priority, L = Low Priority

Cambodia

The two leading organized crime problems in Cambodian are drug trafficking/production and human trafficking. Cambodian officials are concerned that drugs produced in neighboring countries are being trafficked into Cambodia for local consumption. There is also the problem of drug traffickers using Cambodia as a transit country, but Cambodian authorities are less alarmed by this. The trafficking of Cambodian women into Thailand for sex work and the presence of a large number of Vietnamese women in the Cambodian sex industry are major concerns for NGO groups in Asia. According to NGO people in Cambodia, however, local authorities are reluctant to crack down on the local sex industry because they want to promote Cambodia as a place for cheap sex to attract tourists (Gilboa 2001). Some NGO people believe that Cambodian authorities are either directly involved in the sex trade or benefit from it. These same sources indicate that there is no link between terrorism and trafficking in women in Cambodia.

To sum up the perspectives of local authorities, the different countries in Asia clearly have different concerns about organized crime activities (see Table 1). In general, most countries are more concerned with criminal activities that directly impact on their societies, and pay less attention to those activities that they see as only affecting their international images. Human trafficking falls into this latter category. That means their top priorities are mostly traditional organized crime activities committed by local crime groups rather than transnational crime activities involving foreign crime groups. None of our sources (respondents and reports) indicated any strong connections between organized crime and terrorism.

American Authorities' Viewpoint

The American authorities with whom we spoke were much more likely than the Asians to consider transnational organized crime activities to be the more serious organized crime problems in Asia. This could be because their job responsibilities require them to adhere to and represent official U.S. policy on issues such as human trafficking. It could also be because in some cases they lack knowledge and understanding of the local situation, as a result of depending upon formal sources of information. In any event, from the U.S. viewpoint, the problems of drug production and trafficking, human smuggling, trafficking in women and children for the purpose of prostitution, arms trafficking, and money laundering are all very serious problems in Asia. They also think that these activities have either a direct or indirect impact on U.S. interests or, at the very least, that they have undermined the stability and well being of ally countries in Asia.

Some American officials – repeat some – we interviewed thought that the U.S. government is paying too much attention to terrorism, at the expense of transnational organized crime. None of them believe that terrorist groups and transnational organized crime groups are linked. As previously indicated, this is also the view held by some (of those who expressed any opinion on the issue) of the Asian authorities as well. For example, faculty members at the Fuzhou Police College in China (most of whom are former police officers) said there is no collaboration between organized crime and terrorists. In China, Taiwan, and Hong Kong, our correspondents indicated that none of the sixteen organized crime groups they surveyed has shown evidence of involvement in terrorism.

OUR ASSESSMENT

Organized Crime Problems

Based on our interviews, fieldwork, and reading the literature on organized crime in Asia, we think the five leading organized crime problems in Asia (not necessarily in this order) are:

(1) drug production and trafficking;
(2) trafficking in women and children;
(3) human smuggling,
(4) the nexus between organized crime and politics and official corruption,
(5) the penetration into legitimate businesses by organized crime groups.

Because American researchers might encounter many obstacles in studying the last two topics, and because these activities are less likely to have a direct impact on the U.S., we suggest that American resources should be devoted to researching the first three organized crime problems.

Heroin continues to be a popular drug among Asians, and the Golden Triangle in Southeast Asia is still a major heroin-producing area. What is alarming is that heroin traffickers are taking advantage of China's open-door policy and transporting drugs from the Golden Triangle through China (Zhao and Ke 2003). The Chinese land route not only enables traffickers to move hundreds of kilograms of heroin in one delivery, but also helps them to develop a huge heroin market in a country with more than 1.3 billion people. Some heroin traffickers in China are also utilizing the Chinese route to transport large quantities of heroin into the United States (Chu 2004).

The recent development in the production and trafficking of amphetamine is a major problem in China, Taiwan, Japan, and the Philippines. Moreover, the massive production of methamphetamine in the Golden Triangle by the

United Wa State Army and the explosion of methamphetamine use in Thailand are no doubt not only serious problems but are also volatile international problems for two hostile neighbors such as Burma and Thailand. As a result, we think that the use, production, and trafficking of drugs should be considered a serious organized crime problem in Asia.

Putting aside what Asian authorities had to say, we believe that trafficking in women and children for the purpose of prostitution is a very serious problem in Asia (Skrobanek et al. 1997, Williams 1999, Thorbek and Pattanzik 2002). We agree with these authorities that some of the women (as opposed to children) have not been forced, coerced, or deceived into prostitution, but anyone who is familiar with the plight of a large number of women and children engaged in the sex trade in a foreign country will agree that this is a major problem that needs to be addressed. The distinction between smuggling and trafficking, the relative numbers involved, and comparisons of smugglers and traffickers, all need to be addressed with respect to this issue. The same is true of the claim often made by Asian law enforcement authorities that sex workers voluntarily cross national boundaries and continue their occupation simply to increase their income.

We believe that this problem is only going to get worse before it gets better, especially where the trafficking of Chinese and Vietnamese women is concerned. We should not, however, unconditionally accept such emotional labels as "debt-bondage," "sex slaves," and "trafficked victims" that are often prevalent in discussions of this issue (Asia Watch 1993, Atlink 1995, Brown 2000). There are relevant distinctions and nuances that need to be addressed to permit a fuller understanding of the problem and how to most effectively combat it (Kempadoo and Doezema 1998, Murray 1998, Sobieszczyk 2002, Thorbek and Pattanzik 2002).

The smuggling of human beings is also a serious problem in Asia – in some ways more serious than trafficking because of the numbers involved. Every year, a large number of people in Asia go abroad either legally or illegally to earn better wages. Millions of Filipino and Thai people are working overseas, and many of them have been smuggled abroad. The smuggling of Chinese from China to the United States has continued unabated since the early 1990s, and the practice has spread from the original sending community in Fuzhou City to other provinces, especially Zhejiang Province and the three northeastern provinces of Laoling, Jiling, and Heilongjiang. Moreover, the smuggling fee per person has been increased from around $30,000 in the early 1990s to $65,000 after 9/11. We believe that the issue of human smuggling should also be considered a serious crime problem in Asia, and one that has a direct impact on the United States.

Organized Crime Groups

Let us now turn to the many crime groups active in Asia. We think it is important to differentiate genuine, "traditional" organized crime which has hierarchy, turf, continuity and structure, from crime that is organized to exploit current social and economic conditions (Finckenauer and Waring 1998). In Asia and the United States, there are Asian criminal organizations such as the yakuza, the triads, the jaotou, the jao phro, the tongs, and organized gangs that indeed have a name, a turf, a hierarchical structure, restricted membership, and use violence to monopolize their illegal markets (Chin 1996, Lintner 2003). But there are also networks (many networks) of people who are involved in transnational crime on an ad hoc basis that do not have a group name, a territory, or a structure. They act like, and view themselves as, opportunistic businesspeople rather than violent gangsters. People from each of these two worlds may be involved in transnational crime, but our research suggests that it is the latter network groups who are the key players in transnational "organized crime" (Chin 1990, Finckenauer 1996). We think it is also pertinent to discuss this issue while we are examining the leading "organized crime" problems in Asia.

References

Please see the end of Chapter 4 (Page 82) for references for this chapter.

In: Organized Crime, Gangs and Trafficking ISBN: 978-1-61122-829-8
Editors: C. Webb and P. Dobrev

Chapter 3

SCOPE AND PATTERNS OF ORGANIZED CRIME

James O. Finckenauer and Ko-Lin Chin

There are many crime groups in Asia, some of them indigenous and others imported from abroad or formed by foreigners (see Table 1). As with the task of ranking the seriouness of organized crime problems in Asia, the attempt to generalize the scope of each and every organized crime group is also difficult because this may depend on the country, the group, and the product or service involved.

SCOPE

Table 2 shows the scope of organized crime problems in Asia. In general, most traditional organized crime groups (i.e. mafia-like criminal organizations in China, organized gangs and jiatou in Taiwan, triad societies in Hong Kong and Macau, yakuza in Japan, and jao phro in Thailand) are local in scope. Three Chinese organized crime syndicates identified in a recent UN study – the Liu Yong Syndicate, the Zhang Wei Syndicate, and the Liang Xiao Min Syndicate – were all said to be local or at most regional in their scope, and to be without cooperative relationships with other organized crime groups (United Nations Centre for International Crime Prevention 2000:131-135).

Table 1. Organized Crime Groups in Asia

China
1. Crime groups (no structure)
2. Criminal Organizations (some extent of structure)
3. Criminal syndicates bearing triad (mafia) characteristics
4. Triad Mafia) organizations (not yet exist, according to Chinese authorities
5. Foreign-based triad (mafia) organization

Taiwan
1. Organized gangs
2. *Jiatou* (large, well-organized, territorial crime groups)
3. *Juho* (small, loosely-knit, territorial crime groups

Hong Kong
1. Triad societies
2. Organized crime groups formed by PRC Chinese

Macau
1. Triad societies transplanted from Hong Kong
2. Organized crime groups formed by PRC Chinese

Japan
1. Yakuza
2. Organized crime groups formed by PRC Chinese
3. Organized crime groups formed by Koreans

The Philippines
1. Filipino crime syndicates
2. Chinese drug trafficking groups

Thailand
1. *Jao Pho* or Dark Influence Groups (mostly Thai-Chinese)
2. The United Wa State Army
3. Various organized crime groups formed by foreigners

Cambodia
1. Chinese organized crime groups

No doubt, some members of such local/regional organizations may have influence at the national level, but their legal and illegal operations are more likely to be local in nature. An exception to the latter characteristic is yakuza in Japan. A Japanese official told us that yakuza members are very much involved in the trafficking of persons and the operation of sex establishments in Japan. Some members of these various crime groups may also travel to other countries or may be involved in bilateral or multinational criminal activities, but, as mentioned above, they are not key players in transnational criminal activities (Chu 2000, Hill 2003, Zhang and Chin 2003).

A Chinese official in Beijing explained the organized crime/transnational crime connection this way: "According to our law, there are four types of organized crime groups:

(1) criminal groups;
(2) criminal organizations;
(3) black society-like criminal organizations;
(4) black societies.

Table 2. The Scope of Organized Crime Problems in Asia

	Local	National	Bi-lateral	Multi-national
Drug Trafficking				
Heroin			X	X
Amphetamine			X	X
Methamphetamine			X	X
Drug Manufacturing				
Heroin			X	X
Amphetamine			X	X
Methamphetamine			X	X
Trafficking in women/ children for the sex industry			X	X
Trafficking in human beings for the purpose of labor			X	X
Human smuggling			X	X
Kidnapping for ransom		X	X	
Gambling	X			
Prostitution	X	X	X	X
Political-criminal nexus (bribery, corruption, and mafia politics)	X	X		
Penetration into legitimate businesses	X	X		

At this point, we don't yet have black societies, but we expect them to be formed in the very near future. The above mentioned three groups are not involved in transnational crime. That is because these groups are all territorial – their spheres of influence and their activities are restricted to their own turfs. They are not mature enough to establish a transnational crime network." Similarly, the assessments of specific criminal organizations in Taiwan do not indicate any involvement on the part of these groups in transnational crime. The drug market analysis in Taiwan, however, shows that some organized crime groups may be active in the transnational trafficking of the new, synthetic drugs in particular.

In the Philippines, we were told specifically that the transnational "headhunters" who recruit sex workers there are not members of organized crime groups. In Bangkok, a U.S. official expressed some ambivalence on the question of whether members of traditional organized crime groups have been key players in transnational crime: "I feel strongly that transnational criminal activities are committed by highly organized groups, but I can't prove that these groups are linked to, or are the same as, traditional organized crime groups." A Thai official was much less ambivalent: "In Thailand, there are influential groups [organized crime groups] and there are transnational organized groups formed by foreigners. There is not much relationship existing between the influential groups and the transnational organized crime groups."

Even those nontraditional organized crime groups that are heavily involved in transnational crimes such as drug trafficking and human smuggling/trafficking are local or at most national in scope. Their transnational criminal operations are almost always compartmentalized. Most large-scale transnational criminal activities, such as the trafficking of hundreds of kilograms of heroin or the smuggling of hundreds of illegal immigrants, involve numerous independent groups operating in source, transit, and destination countries. There are also, however, mom-and-pop, small-scale transnational criminal activities involving a couple trying to smuggle a small amount of drugs or two or three migrants from one country to another. What is unique about transnational crime is that it can be carried out in some cases by an individual, e.g., computer crime, or by a group or network with hundreds of members or associates (Zhang and Chin 2002).

SPECIALIZATION

Most of our subjects suggest that there is little specialization among traditional organized crime groups. Most of these groups are involved in a variety of both legitimate and illegitimate businesses. While these crime groups continue to be involved in traditional organized crime activities such as gambling, prostitution, drug distribution, loan sharking, debt-collection, conflict mediation, and violence, they are also expanding their influence into legitimate businesses such as the stock market, construction, waste disposal, wholesale markets, and the food industry.

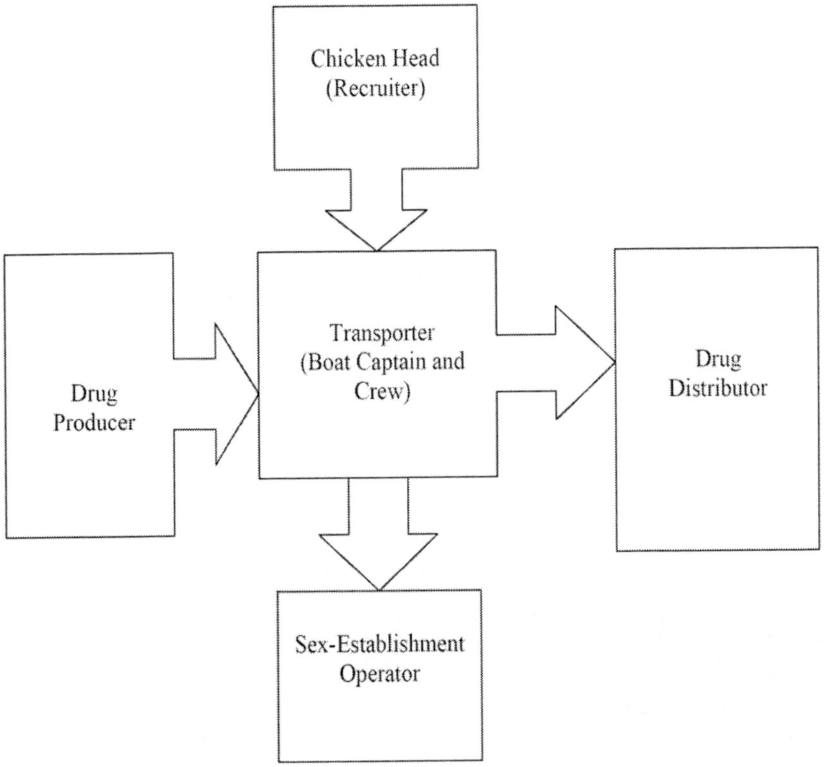

Figure 1. The Intersection between Drug and Human Trafficking across Taiwan Strait

According to our subjects, however, transnational crime networks are highly specialized. It is relatively unlikely for a human smuggling organization to be involved in drug trafficking, or for a drug-manufacturing group to participate in the trafficking of women for prostitution. As we indicated, almost all our subjects also suggest that there is little link between traditional organized crime groups or transnational crime networks and terrorist groups.

The only overlapping or non-specialization that may occur is among offenders who are involved in transportation. In this instance, individual members, as opposed to crime groups as a whole, may crossover in providing services for smuggling and trafficking. As shown in Figure 1, even though there are different groups operating in the source and destination countries in a given transnational criminal activity and these various groups do not get involved in more than one type of transnational crime, the same group responsible for transportation may simultaneously be involved in smuggling both drugs and human beings.

Structure or Opportunity?

Traditional organized crime groups are preexisting groups, while transnational crime networks are developed in response to criminal opportunities. Some of the traditional organized crime groups we mentioned above have been in existence in Asia for centuries and they are most likely to continue to exist. These groups have names, structure, territory, and a strong attachment to their environment, and as a result are handicapped in taking advantage of criminal opportunities that are transnational in nature (Zhang and Chin 2003). The second group, the networks of transnational crime, are more likely to emerge around specific opportunities. Very often, a nuclear or an extended family will initiate an operation in response to a new opportunity and people from the same village or at least the same ethnic group who are living in source, transit, and destination countries will be recruited to participate as members of a network that may dissolve after the criminal operation is successfully carried out.

This distinction has implications for both research and policy. For research, there is a need to expand our current thinking about the causes of organized crime and about the risks and vulnerabilities that may lead to the creation of criminal markets. There is also a need to better understand how those criminal markets operate in order to provide useful information to shape strategies and tactics to disrupt them. For policy, law enforcement officials need to do more thinking “out of the box” of traditional, mafia-like structures in order to effectively combat the crime networks that are dominating transnational organized crime.

THE FLOW

There are several major movement patterns involving sex workers, drugs, and laborers on the transnational scene.

Sex Workers

In Asia, the most notable flows of trafficked women are: (1) from the Philippines to Japan, (2) from Thailand to Japan, (3) from Burma (or Myanmar) to Thailand, (4) from Vietnam to Cambodia, and (5) from Nepal to India. There are also somewhat less notable movements such as (1) from Cambodia to Thailand, (2) from Laos to Thailand, and (3) from the Philippines to Korea.

Our fieldwork in Asia leads us, however, to believe that the most significant development in human smuggling and trafficking is the massive movement of women from China to other Asian countries and, indeed, to the rest of the world. Authorities in all the countries we visited indicate that many Chinese women are showing up in their sex industries; sex establishments in Hong Kong, Taiwan, Macau, and Japan have almost been taken over by Chinese sex workers. The presence of large numbers of Chinese women in the sex industries of Burma, Thailand, Singapore, Malaysia, Indonesia, Australia, and the United States has also been heavily reported.

Drugs

In Asia, heroin is produced in the Burmese part of the Golden Triangle and flows into the international market via either Thailand or China. China's heroin market is expanding rapidly, and heroin markets exist in most Southeast Asian countries and also in Australia. Methamphetamine is produced in the Burmese part of the Golden Triangle as well; Thailand is the main market for the drug. Meth is smuggled into Thailand either across the Burma-Thai border or through Laos and Cambodia. Amphetamine is mainly produced in China and smuggled into Taiwan, Japan, the Philippines, and other Asian countries.

Undocumented Workers

A large number of Chinese laborers are smuggled by boat into Taiwan across the Taiwan Strait. Chinese are also arriving in Japan and Burma in large numbers. The presence of a substantial number of Chinese, both legal and illegal migrants, is also a matter of concern for the majority of nations in Asia. Undocumented workers are also a matter of concern in the United States. And it is to the general issue of impact on the U.S. that we turn in the next section.

REFERENCES

Please see the end of Chapter 4 (Page 82) for references for this chapter.

In: Organized Crime, Gangs and Trafficking ISBN: 978-1-61122-829-8
Editors: C. Webb and P. Dobrev

Chapter 4

THREAT, IMPACT AND HARM TO THE UNITED STATES

James O. Finckenauer and Ko-Lin Chin

As a description and illustration of the impact of Asian organized criminality on the United States, it is important to point out what our discussion does and does not contain. In the latter category, we do not deal with the garden variety of crimes that just happen to have been committed by Asians, nor do we examine the Asian street gangs that operate in certain U.S. cities. Instead, our focus is first upon those crimes that appear to be transnational in nature – the U.S. being on the receiving end – and, that originate in (or at least involve) any of the eight countries (or administrative regions) that were the focal point of our study here. We realize that any gaps in our coverage may be in part a consequence of these choices.

Our second focus requires that we construe impact and harm broadly, to include not only direct criminal activities in the United States, but also harm and/or potential harm to U.S. interests both at home and abroad. For example, given the history and the volatility of relations between mainland China and Taiwan, and the strong U.S. interest and investment in that area, criminal developments involving those entities are of critical interest to the United States. In other cases, where there are developing U.S. business interests, such as in China and in the casino industry in Macau, again there is the potential for a criminal impact on U.S. interests. Such matters are our second focus.

The methods we employed in our research clearly influence our ability to discern the threat, impact, and harm to the U.S. and to U.S. interests, and thus a further word about methodology is in order. As noted, our principal respondents in interviews were nationals (scholars, law enforcement officials, and in some cases victims) of the respective countries that we visited. Thus, their perspective of how, what they know, might impact upon the United States is pretty much speculative. Even in the cases of the U.S. officials that we interviewed in each country, their perspectives on the crime and organized crime problems are an "in-country" view, albeit keeping United States' interests very much in mind.

In addition to the interviews and field visits we conducted, as previously mentioned, we had local scholars in Hong Kong and Taiwan prepare market assessments of the criminal markets of human trafficking and drug trafficking, and also analyses of the major organized crime groups in each of their respective areas. Again, we should recognize that these reflect the perspectives of those native scholars.

None of this should be construed to mean that the interviews, assessments, and analyses are not valuable – quite to the contrary. Our original sources provide a foundation, a stepping off point, to compare and relate what we learn from them, with a plethora of existing secondary materials. We will therefore look at what we learned in the context of what has been recently reported in various U.S. government reports and research studies. The latter include in particular: (1) the U.S. State Department's Trafficking in Persons Report for 2004; (2) "The Commercial Sexual Exploitation of Children in the U.S., Canada and Mexico" (a 2002 report to NIJ by Estes and Weiner); (3) "Sex Trafficking of Women in the United States" (a 2001 report to NIJ by Raymond and Hughes); and (4) a "Survey of Practitioners to Assess the Local Impact of Transnational Crime" (a 2003 report to NIJ by Abt Associates). We also look to the work of Bertil Linter in his 2002 book, Blood Brothers: The Criminal Underworld in Asia. Let us turn first to what we can say about crime impacts directly upon the United States.

Threat, Impact and Harm to the United States

When asked about transnational crime, only a few of our Asian respondents referred to specific crimes impacting the U.S. For example, according to members of the faculty of the Fuzhou Police College in China, the principal forms of transnational crime involving China and the United

States are kidnapping and human trafficking. And, officials of the Bureau of Investigation of the Ministry of Justice of Taiwan, told us that fake IDs are used to gain Taiwanese passports for travel to the U.S. by Chinese who are being smuggled here. But as we showed in Table 1, these are not seen as high priority (or even medium priority for the most part) problems in Asia. On the other hand, as we pointed out earlier, human trafficking and smuggling were indeed high priority issues for most of the U.S. authorities with whom we spoke. These included U.S. officials both in Washington and abroad. For instance, an FBI official indicated that each of such activities as trafficking in women/children for the sex industry, trafficking in human beings for the purpose of labor, and illegal immigration were transnational criminal activities of Chinese organized crime groups in the United States.

Let us begin then with the human trafficking problem. The issues here concern this seemingly vast difference in priority accorded this problem by Asian versus U.S. authorities, substantive differences between smuggling and trafficking, and differences between organized crime and what we call the crimes that are organized. The latter, as we indicated earlier, involve networks of criminal entrepreneurs who exploit criminal opportunities, but who do not have the attributes of traditional organized crime, e.g., continuity, hierarchical structures and leadership, self-identification with the group, multiple criminal enterprises, violence, corruption and government protection, etc. The Asian authorities view what is happening in the transnational movement of people as mostly smuggling. People wanting to leave China, for example, pay smugglers to transport them to Taiwan or even to the United States. There is little or no coercion or deception in these cases. This is part of the reason for the authorities' lack of concern.

Our Asian experts also do not see this smuggling as an activity of traditional organized crime groups. A top criminal investigator with the Ministry of Public Security in Beijing told us that human trafficking was indeed "organized," but that it was not a form of organized crime. He indicated the main destination countries for Chinese women were Japan, Korea, Russia, Taiwan, and Hong Kong. Our correspondent in Hong Kong indicated that in the cases of the three most prominent organized crime groups in Hong Kong (the San Yee On, the Wo Shing Wo, and the 14K), none of the three are involved in human smuggling or human trafficking. Other authorities in Hong Kong likewise told us that there is very limited trafficking in Hong Kong, that the vast majority of people moving trans-nationally are smuggled (not trafficked), and that this is a "mom and pop" industry not controlled by organized crime. These views reflect those of authorities in the other locations we visited as well. For example, representatives of the National Police Administration in Taiwan said there is no evidence of the human smugglers engaging in other transnational organized crime activities, nor are they involved with well-established organized crime groups. In fact, as we said, because the judges in Taiwan do not consider human smuggling to be an activity of organized crime, they do not enforce the Organized Crime Prevention Law against smugglers.

So what is the impact of Asian human smuggling/trafficking upon the United States? Both the United Nations and the United States (in the TIPS report) make much of the connection between organized crime and human trafficking. The latter report concludes that trafficking fuels organized crime. As indicated above, our interviews and examination of the data from the aforementioned reports seem to belie that claim – at least as far as the specific problem of smuggling/trafficking from Asia to the U.S. is concerned.

Seeking some empirical evidence that might shed light on this issue, let us begin with the Raymond and Hughes study that tracked incidents of trafficking to the U.S. between 1990 and 2000. Of 38 specific cases they describe, 18 had an Asian connection, particularly from Thailand or elsewhere in Southeast Asia (Raymond and Hughes, 2001:100-105). From their brief descriptions of these cases, some are clearly alleged to have organized crime involvement, but a dozen or so cases over a ten-year period does not strike one as a huge number. Further, Raymond and Hughes's interview respondents indicated that the trafficking organizations with which they were familiar were mostly small, having only 1-5 people involved. This supports the mom and pop characterization rather than the organized crime one. Since we have used this label several times, what does a "typical" mom and pop case look like? The following is illustrative.

> U.S. federal authorities arrested in Miami a husband and wife team who allegedly smuggled thousands of Chinese illegal immigrants into the United States over the past 20 years. Alexandre Wei, a Taiwanese national with French citizenship, and his wife Bing Xei, a Chinese citizen, used Miami, Florida as the U.S. entry point for their clients, who usually ended their round-the-world journey in New York City. In Manila, U.S. and Philippine authorities arrested the couple's son Jacques, a suspected co-conspirator, along with six other Chinese. This family of people smugglers would first send their clients from China to the Philippines and several other Asian countries. They would then be moved to France, Suriname, or the French territories in the Caribbean, Jamaica or the Bahamas. From the West Indies,

the illegal immigrants were moved to Florida. The illegal immigrants were charged as much as $50,000 each by the smuggling ring.

Tanya Weinbert, Sun-Sentinel (Fort Lauderdale, Florida), November 11, 2003.

Next, the Estes and Weiner study surveyed a variety of sources, including 1,000 informants in 17 U.S. cities, in their examination of the commercial sexual exploitation of children (including trafficking). They concluded that among the "less common" forms of this exploitation was participation by international organized crime networks. Only 10 percent of the children they encountered had been trafficked internationally, and that included from all sources (Africa, Central and Latin America, and Central and Eastern Europe) as well as from Asia (Estes and Weiner, 2002:8). Thus again, these findings do not support a belief that human trafficking to the U.S. by Asian organized crime is a major problem.

Do U.S. law enforcement agencies view human trafficking in general as a critical issue? In a survey of 184 state and local police departments from across the country, Abt Associates asked how many had conducted investigations and made arrests for human trafficking, among a list of transnational crimes. The sources of the trafficking were not delineated, but fewer than a third had conducted investigations, and fewer than a quarter had make arrests in any instances of human trafficking (Abt Associates, 2003). Extrapolating from this, to how much of their activity may have involved Asian organized crime, would again seem to produce relatively small figures. Lest this result be attributed to a belief that this is due to federal law enforcement having jurisdiction over a significant volume of such cases, we offer the following.

We requested from the Justice Department access to all recent federal indictments involving all forms of Asian organized crime. Our request produced eleven RICO indictments of Asian criminals for a variety of crimes in the United States (provided us by the Organized Crime and Racketeering Section of the U.S. Department of Justice). The indictments covered the period 1993 to 2002. We do not claim that these are either all the cases, or that they are a representative sample of all the cases. Instead, they are simply an opportunity sample. Seven of the eleven indictments charged crimes that could be construed to be related to human trafficking, e.g., interstate travel for illegal sexual activities, prostitution, kidnapping and hostage taking, asylum fraud, and alien smuggling.

Perhaps the best known of these cases is the "Sister Ping" case. Chen Chui Ping, who is referred to as "the mother of all snakeheads," allegedly earned $30 million over 15 years transporting thousands of undocumented Chinese into the U.S. To do so, she retained subcontractors in New York and other American cities. These included the notorious Fuk Ching gang in New York, who performed the domestic chore of transporting smuggled Chinese from Boston to New York City. Apart from this connection with a known criminal group, Sister Ping and her operation very much exemplify the kind of entrepreneurial criminal networks we have been describing.

Our first general observation from these cases, with the proviso about representativeness stipulated above, is that seven such cases over a 10-year period again does not appear to be an especially large number. Second, an examination of the details in the indictments indicates that most of these cases involved crimes that were indeed organized by opportunistic networks, e.g., Sister Ping, but not by traditional and well-defined Asian organized crime groups having the characteristics outlined previously. This reinforces our earlier observation that it is the former, rather than the latter, who are the key players in Asian transnational crime.

That we believe that this is a smuggling rather than a trafficking issue, that it is conducted by entrepreneurial criminal networks rather than by traditional OC, and that the estimates of victims and cases may be overstated, does not mean that there is no reason for concern. The Department of Homeland Security estimates that there may be some seven million illegal immigrants living in the U.S., and in FY 2000 alone, 1.8 million illegals were apprehended. We do not know (nor does anyone else) how many of either of these numbers are Asian. What we do assume, however, is that any substantial number is a drain on U.S. resources, accountable to that part of the world. Demands upon education, health care, social services, and for jobs have a financial impact. A specific case in point is reflected in our visit to a village near Fuzhou in China that has been the source of much smuggling of people to the United States. There, we were introduced to a number (35-40) of Chinese children of pre-school age. These children were referred to by our official guide as "citizens," as in U.S. citizens. They were children born in the U.S., now being raised in China until they reach school age, at which point they will return to the U.S. for schooling. The costs of educating these children of parents – many of whom were illegal immigrants -- will obviously have a financial impact upon the U.S.

Impact on U.S. Interests

Irrespective of how much crime emanating from Asia may actually show up on U.S. shores, there are broader U.S. interests at stake here. These interests relate to humanitarian concerns, to business interests, to political relationships, to investments in training and assistance, and to law enforcement cooperation.

The United States does, and very much should have an interest in what happens to trafficking victims and to persons who are being smuggled across national borders. This interest exists apart from the question of how many such persons actually wind up in the U.S. It is a humanitarian and human rights issue. As it does elsewhere in the world, the problem in Asia requires effort and investment on both the demand and supply sides of the human trafficking/smuggling equation. Economic development and opportunity must be coupled with action to combat exploitative sex tourism, corruption, and official indifference.

We have mentioned U.S. business interests previously, e.g., in casinos in Macau and in trade in China and Taiwan. To the extent that the local and regional organized crime in these countries penetrates, interferes with, and jeopardizes business, to that extent that is harmful to U.S. interests. A specific example of this sort of harm is the crime of intellectual property theft, including software piracy. All six of the criminal organizations surveyed in Taiwan and Hong Kong, for example, are reported to be involved in pirated CDs and DVDs. In the case of the Wo Shing Wo, it is said to be the dominant activity in which the group is involved. Our interview of U.S. customs officials in Beijing stressed the problem of intellectual property theft as a major concern.

As it has elsewhere, the United States has made a considerable investment in law enforcement training and assistance in Asia. The U.S., for example, operates the International Law Enforcement Training Academy in Bangkok that has trained hundreds of law enforcement operatives from throughout the region. It is obviously in the best interests of the U.S. to see this investment payoff. Such payoff includes more effective combating of the crime problems we have described here. With respect specifically to drug trafficking, the DEA emphasized to us that China is a critically important player on the Asian drug scene; it was described as the key to heroin trafficking. What is needed, they said, is more joint investigative training and exchanges of intelligence information between the U. S. and China.

On the political front, the United States walks a tightrope balancing our interests in China, Hong Kong, and Taiwan. Because the crime problems we have described are, for the most part, regional problems, they require regional solutions. It is in the U.S. interest to play the role of honest broker in helping the region deal with organized crime.

Finally and specifically, a number of law enforcement officials, particularly in Taiwan and China expressed dissatisfaction with Interpol and with cooperation with U.S. law enforcement. Interpol they regard as basically ineffective. With respect to U.S. cooperation, they complained of essentially being ignored when they make requests for information and assistance. The Mutual Legal Assistance Treaty (MLAT) system was criticized as involving too much "red tape." Whatever the merits of these complaints, they obviously have implications for U.S. efforts to secure information and assistance for its own investigations.

Research on Organized Crime in Asia

As part of our objective to identify potential research partners, we talked to a number of organized crime researchers in Asia about their willingness to collaborate with U.S.-based researchers. Not surprisingly, they all welcomed the opportunity to do so. They also remind us, however, that there are very few resources in their countries to support research and, as a result, it is important for U.S.-based researchers to come up with the financial resources. The following is a list of researchers we met in Asia, their affiliations, and the areas of mutual interest.

China

China Institute of Contemporary International Relations (CICIR)

This institute operates under the auspices of the executive branch of the Chinese central government and thus has the authority to participate in joint research projects with foreign scholars, and most importantly has the connections to collect crime data. We had a meeting with Professor Mingjie Yang, Director/Senior Researcher of the Center for Crisis Management Studies; Director Wei Li, Senior Associate for Research; Gang Shi, Senior Associate for Research; Ying Gao of the Center for Counter-Terrorism Studies; and Program Coordinator Bo Liu of the Division for International

Exchanges. They are interested in conducting studies on the political-criminal nexus in China, and on drug trafficking, human trafficking, and human smuggling.

CICIR proposed jointly (with the U.S.) funded projects that might focus on "academic" research apart from government purposes. By this, we took it to mean not simply studies of topics only of interest to the government. They would be interested in an exchange of delegations, in bi-lateral or multi-lateral conferences, and in some kind of visiting fellows program. They indicated specific interest in comparative research on youth gangs.

People's Public Security University of China

This university is the training ground for high-level law enforcement officers in China and belongs to the Ministry of Public Security (MPS), the all-encompassing law enforcement organization in China. Because crime data are often treated as a state secret in China and interviewing law enforcement authorities is almost impossible for researchers not affiliated with the MPS, it is important that any research on crime in China should involve researchers from this university. We met Professor Dawei Wang and Professor Hongjie Tian of the university while we were in Beijing and both of them are interested in any topic that is related to organized crime. They are very much interested in collaborative research with foreign scholars.

Taiwan

National Central Police University

Like the People's Public Security University in China, the National Central Police University is the key academic institution in Taiwan for training high-ranking police officers. As in China, the collection of crime data is also a challenge in Taiwan and outsiders (meaning professors from purely academic institutions) often do not have access to official statistics or reports. For this reason, we think that it is important to have researchers from the National Central Police University involved in any research projects on organized crime in Taiwan because almost all high-ranking police officers in Taiwan are alumni of this university. We met Professor and Chair Ping-wu Chang, Professor Sandy Yeh, Professor Wen-yung Chou, and Professor Bill Hsu of the School of Crime Prevention and Correction, a major research institute within the university that offers a Ph.D. program in criminal justice. These individuals are interested in issues such as the trafficking of Chinese women into Taiwan for the purpose of prostitution, cross-border drug trafficking between Myanmar and China and its impact on the heroin market in Taiwan, the repatriation of undocumented Chinese from Taiwan to China, and improving cross-strait cooperation between the Chinese and the Taiwanese police forces.

Department of Prosecutorial Affairs of the Ministry of Justice (MOJ)

The Department of Prosecutorial Affairs of the Ministry of Justice (MOJ) should be considered as a potential research partner not only because Director Pi-yu Tsai, Public Prosecutor Chi-jen Ching, Prosecutor Tay-jeng Li, and Liaison Officer Dan Chan of the department are eager to participate in joint research projects with U.S.-based researchers, but because they also have access to most official data on organized crime in Taiwan. The MOJ is mainly interested in such issues as drug trafficking, money laundering, the penetration of organized crime into politics, and ways to improve international law enforcement cooperation.

National Taipei University, Graduate School of Criminology

In addition to the above two institutions, professors at the Graduate School of Criminology, National Taipei University, are also eager to work with U.S.-based scholars. Professor Chuen-jim Sheu, a criminal justice Ph.D. from the State University at Albany, New York, is program chair and an expert on organized crime in Taiwan, and he has said that he will be interested in working with American scholars in any project that is related to organized crime or transnational crime. Professor Sheu was our correspondent for organized crime groups and criminal markets in Taiwan.

Hong Kong

University of Hong Kong (UHK)

The Center for Criminology at the University of Hong Kong is ideally located to conduct research on transnational organized crime activities in Asia. Unfortunately, the center (as a matter of fact, the whole of Hong Kong) has only one criminologist who specializes in organized crime, and that is Professor Yiu Kong Chu (our correspondent in Hong Kong). He is interested in conducting joint research projects on triad societies, human smuggling, human trafficking, and drug trafficking. Another professor at the UHK's Sociology Department is Karen Joe, a U.S.-trained criminologist who has written extensively on street gangs and female involvement in crime. The Centre for Criminology at the University might provide an ideal vehicle for collaborative projects. We met with the then Director of the Centre (David Hodson, who has unfortunately since retired), but who nevertheless was quite optimistic about the possibilities.

Japan

National Research Institute of Police Science

According to our subjects in Japan, there are relatively few criminologists there and none of them specialize in research on organized crime. The largest crime research institution in Japan is the National Research Institute of Police Science, and within it the Department of Criminology and Behavioral Sciences. The director of the department, Dr. Yutaka Harada, is a U.S.-trained criminologist but he said that no one in his department studies organized crime. Nevertheless, he did say his institution was interested in conducting research with American scholars on the issues of organized crime. He also stated that his is the ideal organization to work with if someone wants to collect crime data in Japan.

The Philippines

Philippine Center on Transnational Crime (PCTC)

The center is part of the Philippine National Police (PNP) and researchers at the center are all considered to be law enforcement officials. We talked to Reynold Osia, Police Superintendent and Director; Ireno Bacolod, Police Senior Superintendent and Director; Nolan Antonio, Police Superintendent and Chief of Budget and Finance; and Ernesto Belen, Police Chief Superintendent and Deputy Executive Director of Operations. It is apparent that they are all well-connected to the Philippine criminal justice system. They are interested in collaborating with American researchers in the study of drug trafficking, money laundering, arms smuggling, trafficking in persons, intellectual property rights violations, piracy and armed robbery against ships, cyber-crime, and terrorism.

Philippine Public Safety College

This college is responsible for the education and training of police officers in the Philippines. We met the president of the college, Rosita Evangelista, and several faculty members and a score of high-level police officers who are receiving continuing education at the college. The president is very excited about the possibility of working with American researchers and she said her colleagues would be interested in collaborating on any research topics proposed by U.S. scholars. Of all the countries we have visited, U.S. researchers would have the fewest communication problems in the Philippines because most Filipinos speak fluent English.

Long standing American ties to the Philippines, and humanitarian concerns related to the large outward migration of Filipino workers are compelling reasons for U.S. attention.

Thailand

Thammasat University

This university is considered to be one of the preeminent research institutions in Thailand. Moreover, some of the faculty members of the law school are active in criminological research as well. Professor Prathan Watanavanich and Professor Twekiat Menakanist are well known for their expertise on trafficking in women.

Chulanlongkorn University

Pasuk Phongpaichit, a UK-trained economist at the university, has written extensively on corruption, the illegal economy, and public policy in Thailand. She is well respected and well connected and she should be a very good partner for joint research projects on transnational organized crime in Thailand.

We do not include either Macau or Cambodia for potential research collaborations for several reasons. First, it would be relatively difficult to find research partners in these places and second, Macau and Cambodia could better be studied in concert with researchers from Hong Kong and Thailand. We also do not recommend any NGO organizations in these particular countries because, even though some of the NGOs we talked to are involved in research activities, we do not think they would be ideal research partners. In our view, they are (1) ill-equipped to conduct research; (2) do not have sufficiently well-qualified researchers; and (3) are less likely to be objective because of their stated missions which are advocacy in nature.

From the interviews with researchers and government officials in Asia, we discovered that there is little effort by government agencies in Asia to systematically collect information on organized crime. This means there will not be much that can be readily tapped. We also believe that it is going to be a challenge whenever an American researcher tries to approach government agencies in Asia for access to organized crime data. This, of course, is not unlike the situation in the United States. It is, however, why we emphasized above that American researchers should collaborate with those research partners who can help them gain access to government data. The alternative is for American researchers to plan to collect first hand information from the offenders or the victims instead of relying on secondary, official data.

Structure or Platform to Promote International Research

We recommend three possibilities for pursuing a research agenda on Asian organized crime. There are also other bi-lateral, and/or one-to-one collaborations that can be explored as well. Which of the three main possibilities we describe is adopted will be guided in part by whether the decision is made to pursue a bi-lateral arrangement or a multi-lateral one. An argument in favor of the latter approach is the fact, as we have emphasized, that organized crime in this area has strong regional connotations. The decision on how best to proceed will also be shaped by the degree of participation by U.S. government agencies that is desired.

The most important country to work with, and the best possibility for a bi-lateral arrangement to do so is, we believe, with the China Institute of Contemporary International Relations (CICIR). CICIR appears to have knowledgeable and sophisticated researchers; it has the capability of partnering or working collaboratively with foreign researchers (there are English speakers in the Institute); and, it is well connected to the government. The latter means it has access to data and information that would be critical to research. CICIR is also well regarded for this purpose by U.S. law enforcement representatives in the U.S. embassy in Beijing.

CICIR is interested in joint research funding possibilities, and in developing information for dissemination to the international community. As previously indicated, they are interested in exchanging visiting fellows, and would be interested in considering a formal memorandum of understanding (MOU) with the National Institute of Justice. Besides an interest in the comparative study of youth gangs mentioned earlier, they are interested in examining the differing definitions of organized crime, as they see it, between China and the United States. They are concerned with the huge internal migration from the countryside to the cities in China, and the potential this has for organized crime. They are also, unlike most others with whom we spoke, concerned about links between organized crime and international terrorism.

A specific way to proceed with this particular bi-lateral approach would be to propose a jointly sponsored conference in Beijing on transnational organized crime. This conference might invite specifically, Chinese officials (who CICIR believes are insufficiently aware and concerned about the threats of organized crime), Chinese law enforcement authorities and scholars, U.S. researchers, U.S. law enforcement representatives in China, and members of the diplomatic community. An alternative to moving directly to such a high profile conference could be to first have one or more workshops in which American and Chinese researchers plan and then conduct studies to examine the problems and prepare analyses to be presented at the conference.

A second suggestion, this for a multi-lateral approach, is to pursue a collaboration with the Centre for Criminology at the University of Hong Kong. This would be multi-lateral in that it would involve at least China, Hong Kong, Taiwan, and the United States (other Asian countries could be involved as well). As with the CICIR recommendation, this arrangement could begin either with a major conference, or better yet, with one or more workshops to begin a research collaboration. The advantage of the multi-lateral approach is that it recognizes that organized crime in Asia is very much a regional problem. China and Taiwan are major players with respect to that problem, and Hong Kong provides a "neutral" site for organizing some kind of joint research involving each of them. The enthusiastic support and interest of U.S. law enforcement representatives in Hong Kong would also be a great asset. That said, a major disadvantage is that the Criminology Centre, and the Criminology Program at the University, are vastly under-resourced and under-manned for these purposes. This might require participation by multiple partners – which is certainly possible and who might be sought from the institutions we have identified.

The third possible platform, again beginning with the workshop and then conference idea, is the International Law Enforcement Training Academy in Bangkok. The ILEA has the advantages of being a known regional entity, of being located in a city that itself has significant transnational crime problems, and of providing links to the U.S. law enforcement community (both in Asia and in Washington). The disadvantages might be that it is not geared for this kind of project, would be seen as too U.S.-centric, and might be seen as too oriented to law enforcement as opposed to scholarly research. We regard this as the least preferable of the three possibilities we have outlined.

CONCLUSION

The National Institute of Justice has recognized that crime and criminals more and more have a global face. This recognition means expanding NIJ's international research agenda to both better appreciate and to understand potential threats from transnational crime. We believe that our preliminary assessment of Asian organized crime, our pinpointing of potential research issues of mutual interest, and our identification of potential research partners in Asia lay a solid foundation for that expanded research agenda. We recommend prompt action on our findings and recommendations.

Endnotes

[1] Both the survey and the market analysis were developed by the Center for International Crime Prevention, United Nations Office of Crime Prevention, to assess transnational organized crime worldwide. The instruments were translated into Chinese for the convenience of our Chinese subjects.

REFERENCES (CHAPTERS 2, 3 AND 4)

In English

Abt Associates, Inc. 2003. *Survey of Practitioners to Assess the Local Impact of Transnational Crime.*

Altink, Sietske. 1995. *Stolen Lives: Trading Women into Sex and Slavery. London: Scarlet Press.*

Asia Watch. 1993. *A Modern Form of Slavery: Trafficking of Burmese Women and Girls into Brothels in Thailand.* New York: Human Rights Watch.

Brazil, David. 2004. *No Money, No Honey!: A Candid Look at Sex-for-Sale in Singapore.* Singapore: Angsana Books.

Brown, Louise. 2000. *Sex Slaves: The Trafficking of Women in Asia.* London. Virago Press.

Chin, Ko-lin. 1990. *Chinese Subculture and Criminality: Non-traditional Crime Groups in America.* Westport, CT: Greenwood Pres.

______. 1996. *Chinatown Gangs*. New York: Oxford University Press.

______. 1999. *Smuggled Chinese: Clandestine Immigration to the United States.* Philadelphia: Temple University Press.

______. 2003. Heijin: *Organized, Business, and Politics in Taiwan*. Armonk, NY: M.E. Sharpe.

Chu, Yiu-kong. 2000. *Triads as Business*. London: Routledge.

Emerton, Robyn. 2001. Trafficking of women into Hong Kong for the purpose of prostitution: Preliminary research findings. *Occasional Paper No.3*. Hong Kong: University of Hong Kong.

Estes, Richard and Neil Weiner. 2002. *The Commercial Sexual Exploitation of Children in the U.S., Canada and Mexico.* A Final Report submitted to the National Institute of Justice.

Finckenauer, James. 1996. Russian transnational organized crime and human trafficking. In David Kyle and Rey Koslowski (eds.) *Global Human Smuggling*. Baltimore: John Hopkins University Press: 166-186.

Finckenauer, James and Elin Waring. 1998. *Russian Mafia in America*. Boston: Northeastern University Press.

Gelbard, Robert. 1998. "Burma: The booming drug trade." In Robert Rotberg (ed.) Burma: *Prospects for a Democratic Future*. Washington, D.C.: Brookings Institution Press.

Gilboa, Amit. 2001. *Off the Rails in Phnom Penh: Into the Dark Heart of Guns, Girls, and Ganja.* Bangkok: Asia Books.

Hill, Peter. 2003. *The Japanese Mafia: Yakuza, Law, and the State.* New York: Oxford University Press.

Human Rights Watch. 1995. *Rape for Profit: Trafficking of Nepali Girls and Women to India's Brothels.* New York: Human Rights Watch.

_______. 2000. *Owed Justice: Thai Women Trafficked into Debt Bondage in Japan*. New York: Human Rights Watch.

Jeffrey, Leslie Ann. 2002. *Sex and Borders: Gender, National Identity, and Prostitution Policy in Thailand.* Chiang Mai: Silkworm Boos.

Kaplan, David and Alec Dubro. 2003. *Yakuza: Japan's Criminal Underworld.* Berkeley: University of California Press.

Kempadoo, Kamala and Jo Doezema (eds.) 1998. *Global Sex Workers: Rights, Resistance, and Redefinition.* New York: Routledge.

Kwong, Peter. 1997. *Forbidden Workers: Illegal Chinese Immigrants and American Labor*. New York: The New Press.

Lintner, Bertil. 2003. *Blood Brothers: The Criminal Underworld of Asia*. New York: Palgrave McMillan.

Lo, T. Wing. 1993. *Corruption and Politics in Hong Kong and China.* Buckingham: Open University Press.

Murray, Alison. (1998). Debt-bondage and trafficking: Don't believe the hype. In Kamala Kempadoo and Jo Doezema (eds.) *Global Sex Workers: Rights, Resistance, and Redefinition.* New York: Routledge: 51-64.

Pearson, Elaine. 2002. *Human Traffic, Human Rights: Redefining Victim Protection*. London: Anti-Slavery International.

Phongpaichit, Pasuk and Sungsidh Piriyarangsan. 1994. *Corruption and Democracy in Thailand.* Chiang Mai: Silkworm Books.

Phongpaichit, Pasuk, Sungsidh Piriyarangsan, and Nualnoi Teerat. 1998. *Guns, Girls, Gambling, Ganja: Thailand's Illegal Economy and Public Policy.* Chiang Mai: Silkworm Books.

Raymond, Janice and Donna Hughes. 2001. *Sex Trafficking of Women in the United States*. A Final Report submitted to the National Institute of Justice.

Santos, Aida. 2002. *Patterns, Profiles and Health Consequences of Sexual Exploitation: The Philippine Report.* Manila: Coalition Against Trafficking in Women (CATW).

Skrobanek, Siripon, Nattaya Boonpakdi, and Chutima Janthakeero. 1997. *The Traffic in Women: Human Realities of the International Sex Trade.* London: Zed Books.

Sobieszczyk, Teresa. 2002. Risky business: Debt bondage international labour migration from Northern Thailand. Paper presented at the IUSSP Regional Population Conference on *"Southeast Asia's Population in a Changing Asian Context,"* Bangkok, Thailand, 10-12 June.

Smith, Paul (ed.) 1997. *Human Smuggling*. Washington, DC: Center for Strategic and International Studies.

Takano, Hideyuki. 2002. *The Shore Beyond Good And Evil*: A Report From Inside Burma's Opium Kingdom. Reno, NV: Kotan Publishing.

Thorbek, Susanne and Bandana Pattanzik (eds.) 2002. *Transnational Prostitution: Changing Global Patterns.* London: Zed Books.

United Nations Centre for International Crime Prevention. 2000. Overview of the 40 criminal groups surveyed. *Trends in Organized Crime* Vol. 6, No. 2: 93-140.

U.S. Department of State. 2004. *Trafficking in Persons Report*.

van Kemenade, Willem. 1997. *China, Hong Kong, Taiwan, Inc*. New York: Alfred A. Knopf.

Williams, Phil (ed.) 1999. *Illegal Immigration and Commercial Sex: The New Slave Trade.* London: Frank Cass.

Zhang, Sheldon and Ko-lin Chin. 2002. Enter the dragon: Inside Chinese human smuggling organizations. *Criminology* Vol. 40(4): 737-768.

______. 2003. The declining significance of triad societies in transnational illegal activities. *British Journal of Criminology* 43/3: 463-482.

In Chinese

Chang Tseng-liang. 2002. A study on the problem of "fake marriage" across the Taiwan Strait, focusing on fake marriage for the purpose of prostitution. *Central Police University Journal of Police Science* Vol. 33, No. 1: 203-236.

Chu Ping. 2004. *Drug Baron: Corruption in Fujian*. Hong Kong: Sheffield Press.

He Bingsong. 2002. Organized Crime in China. Beijing: China Legal Press.

_______. 2003. *Understanding Organized Crime Activities*. Beijing: China Judicial Press.

Luo Bingsen and Liang Jin-yun. 1999. *Essays on the Suppression of Drug in Yunnan.* Beijing: Qunzhong Publication.

Ma Mo-jen. 1994. *Drugs in China*. Taipei: Kenin Publishing.

Si Yi. 2004. *Sex in China*. Hong Kong: Limited Publisher.

Tse Ping (ed.). 2003. The Power and Sex Trade in China. Hong Kong: Sheffield Press.

Xiao Chong (ed.). 2002. *Chinese Communist and Organized Crime*. Hong Kong:

Sheffield Press.

Zhao Shi-lung and Ke Su-ya. 2003. *Golden Triangle: A Future without Heroin?* Beijing: Economic Daily Publisher.

In: Organized Crime, Gangs and Trafficking ISBN: 978-1-61122-829-8
Editors: C. Webb and P. Dobrev

Chapter 5

TAIWAN GANGS

James O. Finckenauer and Ko-Lin Chin

THE UNITED BAMBOO GANG

I. Organizational Structure

I.1. Internal Hierarchy and/or Division of Labor

The Bamboo United has a headquarters and numerous local branches. According to a 1985 sentencing report, the headquarters is made up of an "Ultimate Gang Leader" (or "Headquarters' Leader" or "Boss"), an "Ultimate Enforcer," and an "Ultimate Superintendent." Various police reports have also suggested that there is an "Ultimate Executive" in the headquarters. The Ultimate Gang Leader leads the gang, the Ultimate Enforcer enforces gang rules, the Ultimate Superintendent monitors gang members and their activities, and the Ultimate Executive operates gang businesses. In 1981, the gang established its first eight branches: Chung (loyalty), Shao (filial pity), Len (sympathy), Eia (love), Shing (trust), Yi (righteousness), Hor (harmony), and Ping (peace). By 1996, there were 21 branches and currently there are more than 60 branches. A branch or a tong has a Branch Leader, Deputy Branch Leader, and "brothers" (or members). Some branches (such as the Ho Tong) also have a Right-arm Enforcer, Left-arm Enforcer, Communication Officer, War Officer, and Internal Regulator. Recently, some branches have had their own sub-branches and some of the sub-branches are "guardian unit" or "combat unit" in nature. Even though there are many branches in the Bamboo United, most of these branches are located in urban centers, especially Taipei City and Taipei County. Branches are often involved in intra-gang conflicts; for example, Ho Tong and Sky Dragon Tong have fought over debt-collection; and Air Tong and Heaven and Earth Tong got involved in a nasty war as a result of a minor argument.

I.2. Ability of the Group to Recruit or Diversify its Human Resources

On March 25, 1999, the police found out that the Ping Tong was involved in the recruitment of more than 40 junior high school students in Shing Tien [a suburban area of Taipei]; on April 18 of the same year, law enforcement authorities discovered that the Sky Eagle Tong was recruiting trade school students in Taipei City and County. This method of massive recruitment of students or drop-outs enables the gang to expand quickly in a short period of time; however, how long these students and drop-outs will belong to the gang is questionable. It is the regular members or those with a long criminal record who are the core of the gang, and it is they who have had the most impact on the gang's development. According to official records, between 2002 and 2004, the number of United Bamboo members who are on the official "watch list" increased by only a mere 100 members.

I.3. Rules and Conditions of Group Membership and Internal Codes of Conduct

There are no specific requirements to become a member. For example, according to police records, Lin Jun-hung became a member of the gang after he met Chen Chi-li [the Ultimate Leader] and Wu Tun (the Ultimate Enforcer) in a prison. There was neither an initiating ceremony nor a formal registration. Over the past few years, the gang has been very active in recruiting students and according to the police, the gang did not have any requirements for the new recruits. A recent study conducted by the National Police University indicated that newly recruited Bamboo United members interviewed said they became members after hanging out with other United Bamboo members for a certain period of time or being introduced into the gang by friends. They also said there was no screening, no special requirements, nor initiation ceremony.

The gang's regulations, written in 1957, require members to:

(1) pay most of their attention to the fight with the Four Seas gang,
(2) not betray the gang,
(3) be united,

(4) contribute NT$5 [about 15 cents] a week to the gang coffers.

Later, as the gang began to expand, different branches sometimes developed their own regulations. For example, the Central Tong's regulations are:

(1) parents are number one;
(2) "brothers" are number two,
(3) do not resist your superiors, follow the orders,
(4) do not use drugs,
(5) do not steal or rob,
(6) do not rape,
(7) do not use your gang name to solve personal problems.

I.4. Primary Mechanisms for Internal Conflict Resolution with Regard to Territorial and Market Division and other Disputes

For the Bamboo United, market division is primarily based on (1) the kinds of businesses existing within a branch's territory and (2) the kinds of businesses branch leaders are familiar with. When there is conflict between two branches, the first priority is to sit down and talk it out, and if this does not work, to try to discuss it peacefully with the help of a senior leader of the gang. If the negotiations break down, then there will be serious violence between branches even though they all belong to the same gang.

II. Violence

II.1. Willingness to Engage in Ruthless Violence

There is both inter-gang and intra-gang violence. The main function of intra-gang violence is to control gang members' behaviors and the main purpose of inter-gang violence is to neutralize the power of rival gangs or to carry out certain gang activities and missions. Bamboo United has often been involved in conflicts with other gangs. For example, in November 2002, the United Bamboo, the Pine Union, the Four Seas allied with the Heavenly Alliance's Sky Eagle Branch to smuggle a large amount of firearms into Taiwan to go to war with the Heavenly Alliance's Sun Branch. At the end of 2003, the United Bamboo's Mei Hua Tong and the Heavenly Alliance's Er Lin Branch got into a shootout after they were unable to settle a business dispute between two groups of legitimate businessmen. The United Bamboo is a heavily armed gang, and members of the gang have often been involved in gun fights with members of rival gangs and jiaotou groups.

II.2. Availability of Enforcers/Specialists in the Use of Violence

Violent acts by the United Bamboo are committed by members of the gang, especially by members of the tongs' guardian unit or combat unit. We have not seen the gang hiring outsiders (hit men or specialists) to commit violence for the gang.

II.3. Access to a Variety of Weapons

The main weapons of the gangs in Taiwan are guns. It is very common for each and every tong to have guns. When gang members are involved in gang conflicts or violent crime, they almost always use guns. Because gun control is relatively tight in Taiwan, gangs in Taiwan also produce their own guns. For example, the United Bamboo's Wang Tong used to own a gun factory where eight re-assembled handguns, manuals, and machines were found.

III. Economic Resources

III.1. Original Source of Capital Accumulation

The United Bamboo's original source of capital accumulation was from traditional organized crime activities. In the 1980s, the gang was involved in extortion, debt-collection, gambling, demanding protection money, prostitution, and operating illegal electronic games.

III.2. Subsequent Diversification of Activities

The gangs in Taiwan were able to accumulate a substantial amount of wealth after the 1980s when the Taiwanese economy took off. In the 1990s, besides continuing to be involved in traditional organized crime activities, the gangs began to penetrate into the legitimate business sector, including providing security, investing in legitimate businesses, bid rigging, construction, investment, mass communication, futures trading, underground banking, publication, entertainment, the movie industry, and cable television, etc.

III.3. Degree of Dominance in Selected Illegal Markets

The Bamboo United has a strong influence over gambling, debt-collection, protection, ecstasy sales, the bar business, fake VCD sales, and the funeral business in Taiwan.

III.4. Degree of Professional Know-How within the Group Itself

Some United Bamboo members own and operate legitimate businesses. However, according to a recent study conducted by the National Police University, police records, and media reports, the level of professionalism within the gang is not as high as the public had imagined. According to the National Police University study, there was not even a lawyer, an accountant, or a professional involved in an entire tong. The tong is nothing more than a big brother mingling with a group of young men just to get by.

IV. Political Resources

IV.1. Corruption and/or Inflation of the Law Enforcement Process

There are very few reports in the news media about the corruption of law enforcement officials by United Bamboo members. The most recent incident involved a case that occurred in October 2003 where local police officers provided information on fugitives to United Bamboo members who were involved in debt-collection. However, from academic studies, there is evidence that there are local police officers demanding bribes from sex establishments operated by gangs.

IV.2. Manipulation of Political Parties Participating in Local and/or National Government

By providing help to political candidates during elections, the gang established a close relationship with politicians so that these politicians will provide the gang with immunity from police crackdowns or help the gang to expand their spheres of influence. For example, gang members help politicians to run for the legislature, city and county councils, town and township representing bodies, and ward chieftains during elections by donating money, participating in campaign activities, and providing protection.

IV.3. Direct Representation in Parliament, Executive or Diplomatic Service

Some of the members used to work as assistants to legislators.

IV.4. Alliance with Armed Opposition Groups

This has not ever happened before.

V. Response of Law Enforcement Agencies to Organized Crime

V.1. Re-Structuring of Law Enforcement Agencies and Operations because of Organized Crime

The Organized Crime Prevention Law was passed on December 11, 1996. Besides having a mechanism with the U.S. to extradite fugitives, the Taiwanese government also has worked with the Chinese authorities on extradition. There are also informal relationships existing between authorities in Taiwan and authorities in Southeast Asia so that fugitives who flee to these countries can be extradited to Taiwan on a case by case basis.

V.2. Changed Law Enforcement Techniques

Local police agencies are actively involved in collecting gang intelligence and this information is provided to the Criminal Investigation Bureau (CIB) to enter into a gang data base and the data base is used by investigators when they investigate gang-related crime. In addition, law enforcers can obtain the approval of the court to monitor the telecommunication activities of suspected gang members.

V.3. Changes in Law because of Organized Crime

The Organized Crime Prevention Law was adopted on December 11, 1996 and this law allows the authorities to confiscate gang members' illegally gained assets. The law also enables authorities to punish gang crime offenders severely, protect witnesses, protect victims and prohibit gang members from running for public offices. Other related laws include:

A. Witness Protection Law (adopted on February 29, 2000)

1. To protect witnesses in criminal cases and hoodlum cases.
2. When witnesses run the risk of physical or financial harms due to their willingness to testify in court, the judge or the prosecutor will issue a witness protection certificate to the witnesses. If the certificate cannot be issued in time, other necessary measures will be adopted to protect witnesses.

B. Money Laundering Law (passed on October 23, 1996)

This law was adopted to punish those who accumulate wealth through major criminal acts, including the development of, participation in, or assisting of organized crime groups. Financial institutions are required under the law to report suspicious financial transaction activities to the designated authority.

C. Anti-hoodlum Law (revised on April 4, 2004)

VI. The External Environment

VI.1. Present Level of Cultural Acceptance of the Group/Organization's Activities in the Social Environment in which They Operate

Ordinary people in Taiwan normally have a negative attitude towards organized gangs, especially when these gangs are involved in violence and politics. However, a small proportion of the general public also want to receive the gangs' services or goods: gambling, prostitution, drugs, debt-collection, etc. As a result, some people are receptive to gangs and may even do business with them.

VI.2. Presence of Social Movement Engaged in Awareness Raising Campaigns on Organized Crime

No such campaigns have ever been carried out in Taiwan.

VI.3. Role of the Press and other Mass Media in Sensitizing Citizens on the Dangers and Threats Posed by Organized Crime on the Society at Large

People in Taiwan generally pay attention to media reports on organized crime, especially during election times or when the gangs penetrate into schools.

HEAVENLY ALLIANCE

I. Organizational Structure

I.1. Internal Hierarchy and/or Division of Labor

In 1984, Taiwanese authorities launched a nationwide gang sweep, code-named Operation Cleansweep, because of rampant gang activities. Many gang members were arrested and sent to prisons for rehabilitation. In the prisons, native Taiwanese gangsters banded together to protect themselves from members of the United Bamboo, a gang whose members were primarily descendants of mainland Chinese who came to Taiwan after 1949. In 1986, at the Taipei Detention Center, under the leadership of the spiritual leader Lo Fu-chu, Lin Min-teh (aka Min-teh), Hsieh Tung-yun (aka Ah-pu-tou), Lee Por-shi, and Chen Hsien-ming (aka Ya-ba) declared the establishment of the "Heavenly Alliance." Many of the participants in the ceremony were assigned as heads of various branches. At that time, Hsiao Jer-hung (aka Ji-kung) announced his intention to join the Heavenly Alliance, and even though he did not participate in the ceremony because he was locked up in the Taipei Prison, he was also allowed to become a branch leader. Thus, at the very beginning, there were six branches under Lo Fu-chu: Sun Branch (Wu Tung-tang as leader), Pu Tou Branch (Hsieh Tung-yun as leader), Ming-the Branch (Lin Ming-the as leader), Peacock Branch (Lee Por-shi as leader), Le Yi Branch (also known as Ya Ba Branch, Chen Hsien-ming as leader), and Cloud Branch (also known as Ji Kung Branch, Hsiao Jer-hung as leader). By 1996, the gang had altogether 14 branches, and it was increased to more than 30 branches in the year 2004. The structure of the most typical branch – the Sun Branch – is as follows: Under the leadership of the Branch Leader, there are Deputy Branch Leaders, Advisers, Special Combat Teams, Unit Chiefs, and members. The deputy branch leaders control the sub-branches and they have the authority to recruit their own unit chiefs. The latter are responsible for expanding their organization and they are the key players in the recruitment of ordinary members. Unit chiefs are free to recruit members as they see fit and need not obtain approval from branch leaders and deputy leaders. Unit chiefs will ask the leaders for instructions or support only when there are major incidents. Even though there are many branches in the gang, some branches are formed as a result of internal struggle, take Unity Branch for example. However, of all the internal conflicts, the war between the new and old Sun Branch is the most violent.

I.2. Ability of the Group to Recruit or Diversify its Human Resources

Under the guidance of the Sun Branch's leader Wu Tung-tang, the Heavenly Alliance gang expanded rapidly as many new members joined the gang. Over the past few years, gangs in Taiwan were eager to have more branches and members to extend their influence. As a result, the Heavenly Alliance also imitates the recruiting tactics of the United Bamboo and the Four Seas, and that is to recruit a large number of students or school drop-outs. For example, a branch of the gang was subject to crackdown by the police in

Yunlin County in 2004 for recruiting students and school drop-outs. This method of massive recruitment of students or drop-outs enables the gang to expand quickly in a short period of time; however, it is also questionable how long these students and drop-outs will remain with the gang. It is the regular members or those with a long criminal record who are the core of the gang, and it is they who have had the most impact on the gang's development and social order. According to official records, between 2002 and 2004, the number of Heavenly Alliance members who are on the official "watch list" increased by only 140 members.

I.3. Rules and Conditions of Group Membership and Internal Codes of Conduct

The gang does not conduct an elaborate initiation ceremony for new recruits. A person becomes a member by simply taking a pledge. According to police intelligence, the gang has four rules: (1) help heaven in dispersing justice, that is to support the weak and help the poor; (2) be honest and candid with other members, that is to be united, (3) follow the example of heaven and earth, that is to assist the world with empathy and justice, and (4) fly as high as possible, that is to travel around the world and do just things. When the police arrested members of the gang's Heaven Snail Branch on March 2004, they discovered that this branch has its own rules, including: members who make a key contribution to the branch cause will receive a monetary reward; members who commit mistakes will be reprimanded or fired; follow orders and do not disobey superiors; do not fight own members for money; do not go out and create trouble; be low key when dealing with outsiders; attend all the branch meetings (if one must be absent, inform the leader); and do not seduce your leader's wife or girlfriend. Like other traditional large gangs, when a gang has many branches, eventually each branch will come up with its own rules.

I.4. Primary Mechanisms for Internal Conflict Resolution with Regard to Territorial and Market Division and other Disputes

The Heavenly Alliance has branches throughout Taiwan, and every branch develops its own economic activities. For economic reasons, members of a branch may become involved in a power struggle. For example, there were conflicts between the Unity Branch and the Sun Branch, and there were shootouts between New and Old factions of the Sun Branch. The Unity Branch was formed mainly to fight the Sun Branch. Even the Sun Branch eventually split into New and Old Sun Branch and they became involved in a bloody war.

The leader of the New Sun Branch was later killed by members of the Old Sun Branch.

II. Violence

II.1. Willingness to Engage in Ruthless Violence

The Heavenly Alliance is heavily-armed and members are willing to use violence when there is a conflict of interests. Members of the gang are often involved in intragang violence. For example, there was a major conflict between the Unity Branch and the Sun Branch, and there were bloody conflicts between the Old and New factions of the Sun Branch. In addition, the gang was involved in intergang violence. For example, members of the gang shot and killed the leader of the Three Rings gang, the gang got involved in a major conflict with the Bamboo United in August 2002 because of the conflict in futures trading, and in 2003 there was a major war between the Heavenly Alliance's Er Lin Branch and United Bamboo's Mei Hua Tong because of a fallout from a failed business dispute. Moreover, members of the Heavenly Alliance set fire to a rival gang's dance hall, kidnapped a legislator by the name of Liao Hsuer-kwang, destroyed the office of Next Magazine, etc. All these incidents indicate that the gang is a violent organization.

II.2. Availability of Enforcers/Specialists in the Use of Violence

Gang-related violent activities are carried out by members. Over the past few years, there were several major violent incidents involving the gang, and judging from these cases, it is clear that the gang does not hire hitmen or killers from the outside.

II.3. Access to a Variety of Weapons

The main weapons for gangs in Taiwan are guns. All the branches of the Heavenly Alliance regularly commit crimes with guns, especially when there is intergang conflict or gang members are involved in violent crime. The gang's Heaven Eagle Branch, working with the Bamboo United, Pine Union, and Four Seas, was involved in gun smuggling to fight against the gang's Sun Branch. The authorities seized 10 handguns and 8,000 rounds of ammunition after a raid in November 2002. On March 2004, the gang's Heaven Snail Branch was found to be involved in operating a gun factory.

III. Economic Resources

III.1. Original Source of Capital Accumulation

At the beginning, the gang was active in providing protection to sex establishments, operating high-stakes gambling operations, and operating a lottery game. After the gang began to be involved in the lottery game, it was able to take over the business across Taiwan. The gang's dominance in the lottery business was originally its main financial source.

III.2. Subsequent Diversification of Activities

After the gang began to grow, each and every branch started its own businesses. The Sun Branch is an example. The branch was involved in operating: nightclubs, dance halls, jewelry stores, a construction consultant company, cable companies, bid rigging, advertising firms, private investigation offices, car washes, furniture stores, newspapers and ecstasy sales. Other branches are active in: loan sharking, restaurants, construction, debt-collection, waste disposal, and prostitution and gambling.

III.3. Degree of Dominance in Selected Illegal Markets

This gang is relatively dominant in the following criminal markets: gambling, prostitution, debt-collection, bid rigging, illegal futures trading, vice, waste land disposal, protection rackets, and extortion.

III.4. Degree of Professional Know-How within the Group Itself

All the branches of the gang operate one or more firms, but these firms are basically fronts for their illegal activities, especially the gang's construction firms. According to various academic researchers, members of the gang are not as professional as the media has depicted. Most of them go after risky and lucrative businesses and use violence to achieve their goals.

IV. Political Resources

IV.1. Corruption and/or Inflation of the Law Enforcement Process

There is very little reported in the news media about the corruption of law enforcement officials by Heavenly Alliance members. However, from academic studies, there is evidence that there are local police officers demanding bribes from sex establishments operated by gangs.

IV.2. Manipulation of Political Parties Participating in Local and/or National Government

Local politicians in Keelung are keenly aware of the influence of the Sun Branch in their jurisdiction. Members of the gang who are in Panchiao often help local politicians to win elections. Some candidates will also pay the gang to help them with their campaigns. Former legislator Lo Fu-chu played a key role in the development of the gang. When Lo was in the legislature, his influence in the congress was immense.

IV.3. Direct Representation in Parliament, Executive or Diplomatic Service

Lo Fu-chu [the gang's spiritual leader] is a former legislator, and his two sons are also successful politicians. At the age of 30, the elder son Lo Ming-shiu was elected to the provincial assembly in the 1990s, making him the youngest assemblyman. The younger son Lo Ming-jia became the youngest national representative at the age of 26, also the youngest KMT central committee member. He won during the 1996 legislature election.

IV.4. Alliance with Armed Opposition Groups

This has never occurred.

V. Response of Law Enforcement Agencies to Organized Crime

See the same section in the report on the Bamboo United.

VI. The External Environment

See the same section in the report on the Bamboo United.

Four Seas Gang

I. Organizational Structure

I.1. Internal Hierarchy and/or Division of Labor

The gang has three types of leaders at the top: "chairman of the committee," "deputy chairman of the committee," and "standing committee members." These leaders are in charge of a number of tongs that belong to the Four Seas. A tong has a tong master, a deputy tong master, "big brothers," and "brothers." The chairman is the ultimate leader of the gang, the deputy chairman is the second in command, and the standing committee members are elected by gang members to represent them in gang meetings to discuss important matters. Decisions made at the meetings are relayed to the tongs to be implemented. In 1997, the Four Seas had only 11 tongs. After rapidly developing for the past several years, there are now more than 40 tongs that are being targeted by law enforcement authorities.

I.2. Ability of the Group to Recruit or Diversify its Human Resources

The Four Seas gang is very good at recruiting new members. For example, when police cracked down on the gang's Heiteh tong in Taichung City in 1995, the authorities found out that the tong had 87 members, even though it was established for only two years at that time. In addition, the tong had 14 underage members. On March 18, 1993, police discovered the Four Seas' Heikung tong recruited more than 20 high school students in Taipei City. The problem with recruiting high school students or drop-outs is that many of them may not remain with the gang for long. It is the regular members or those with a long criminal record who are the core of the gang, and it is they who have had the most impact on the gang's development. According to official records, between 2002 and 2004, the number of Four Seas members who are on the official "watch list" increased by only about 50 members.

I.3. Rules and Conditions of Group Membership and Internal Codes of Conduct

There are no special requirements for new recruits. However, some branches may set up their own methods of recruitment. For example, according to police records, the Heiteh tong will put new recruits on a three-month probationary period. Those who fit in will remain with the tong and those who do not will be asked to leave. The initiation ceremony of the gang has these processes: opening the ceremony, bowing to Kuan Kung [a legendary warrior idolized by the Chinese underworld], taking oaths, pricking fingers, drinking wine mixed with blood, announcing gang rules, and introducing new recruits to old members. There are ten gang rules, all involving the prohibition of : (1) drug use, (2) rape and kidnapping, (3) eating free meals, (4) creating trouble, (5) cheating and fraud, (6) resisting orders, (7) robbery and theft, (8) victimizing good people, (9) compromising national interests, and (10) betraying the gang and its members.

I.4. Primary Mechanisms for Internal Conflict Resolution with Regard to Territorial and Market Division and other Disputes

For the Four Seas, market division is primarily based on (1) the kinds of businesses existing within a branch's territory and (2) the kinds of businesses branch leaders are familiar with. Basically, each and every tong is doing its own businesses independently. When there is conflict between two tongs or branches, the first priority is to sit down and talk it out, and if this does not work, to try to discuss it peacefully with the help of a senior leader of the gang. If the negotiation breaks down, then there will be serious violence between branches even though they all belong to the same gang.

II. Violence

II.1. Willingness to Engage in Ruthless Violence

There is both inter-gang and intra-gang violence. The main function of intra-gang violence is to control gang members' behaviors and the main purpose of inter-gang violence is to neutralize the power of rival gangs or to carry out certain gang activities and missions. Four Seas has often been involved in conflicts with other gangs. For example, in November 2002, the United Bamboo, the Pine Union, and the Four Seas allied with the Heavenly Alliance's Sky Eagle Branch to smuggle a large amount of firearms into Taiwan to go to war with the Heavenly Alliance's Sun Branch. Moreover, according to academic research and police records, the Four Seas have often been involved in violent confrontations with other gangs such as the United Bamboo, Heavenly Alliance, and various jiaotou groups. Members of the gang also use violent tactics such as threats, damaging property, shooting, and assault to achieve their goals. For example, on August 2002, a group of Four Seas members shot and wounded a non-cooperative telecommunications businessman.

II.2. Availability of Enforcers/Specialists in the Use of Violence

Violent acts by the Four Seas are committed by members of the gang, especially by "killers" in the various tongs. We have not seen the gang hiring outsiders (hit men or specialists) to commit violence for the sake of the gang.

II.3. Access to a Variety of Weapons

The main weapons of the gangs in Taiwan are guns. It is very common for each and every tong to have guns. When gang members are involved in gang conflicts or violent crime, they almost always use guns. Police authorities once confiscated an assault rifle from a Four Seas tong. A tong master was arrested and sentenced to jail for working with a Heavenly Alliance member to import firearms into Taiwan. Because gun control is relatively tight in Taiwan, the Four Seas also used altered guns. The gang's Heilun tong and Lenai tong had their own underground firearms manufacturing factories.

III. Economic Resources

III.1. Original Source of Capital Accumulation

The Four Seas's original source of capital accumulation, like other traditional organized gangs, was from traditional organized crime activities, including protection, debt-collection, gambling, prostitution, and extortion.

III.2. Subsequent Diversification of Activities

The gangs in Taiwan were able to accumulate a substantial amount of wealth in the 1980s when the Taiwanese economy took off. In the 1990s, besides continuingd to be involved in traditional organized crime activities, the gangs began to penetrate into the legitimate business sector, including entertainment, underground banking, investment companies, land development, real estate brokerage, bid rigging, and other small businesses.

III.3. Degree of Dominance in Selected Illegal Markets

The Four Seas have a strong influence over gambling, debt-collection, protection, ecstasy sales, bid rigging, fake VCD sales, underground banking, the taxi business, and the waste disposal business in Taiwan.

III.4. Degree of Professional Know-How Within the Group Itself

Even though the gang is engaged in bid rigging, credit card frauds, and price-fixing in the home gas business, according to police records and media reports, the level of professionalism within the gang is not as high as has been imagined. According to the National Police University study, there was not even a lawyer, an accountant, or a professional involved in an entire tong. The operating principles of the gang are opportunistic and violent.

III.5. Degree to Which Some Members of the Group Work Primarily in the Legitimate Economy

Some members of the gang are operating taxi companies, bars, investment companies, real estate companies, car washes, and restaurants.

IV. Political Resources

IV.1. Corruption and/or Inflation of the Law Enforcement Process

There is very little reported in the news media about the corruption of law enforcement officials by Four Seas members. However, from academic studies, there is evidence that there are local police officers demanding bribes from sex establishments operated by gangs.

IV.2. Manipulation of Political Parties Participating in Local and/or National Government

By providing help to political candidates during elections, the gang established a close relationship with politicians so that these politicians will provide the gang with immunity from police crackdowns or to help the gang to expand their sphere of influence. For example, gang members will help politicians to run for the legislature, city and county councils, town and township representing bodies, and ward chieftains during elections by donating money, participating in campaign activities, and providing protection.

IV.3. Direct Representation in Parliament, Executive or Diplomatic Service

Some of the members are elected as city or county councilors.

IV.4. Alliance with Armed Opposition groups

This has not ever happened before.

V. Response of Law Enforcement Agencies to Organized Crime

See the same section in the report on the Bamboo United.

VI. The External Environment

See the same section in the report on the Bamboo United.

In: Organized Crime, Gangs and Trafficking ISBN: 978-1-61122-829-8
Editors: C. Webb and P. Dobrev

Chapter 6

Hong Kong Gangs

Yiu Kong Chu[*]
Department of Sociology, The University of Hong Kong, Hong Kong

San Yee On

1. Background

According to police records, only 14 out of the 50 triad societies remain active in Hong Kong. Out of these 14 active groups, San Yee One is regarded as one of the most influential triad groups. It was originally formed by a Chinese minority native group called Chiu Chau in Hong Kong. Nowadays members of San Yee On come from different ethnic Chinese groups. A small number of local born Indian and Pakistan are also recruited to the Society. Nevertheless, San Yee On is still a male dominant secret society. Few females joined the Society formally.

2. Organizational Structure

It is true that triad societies are secret organizations, but they are in fact loose cartels consisting of a number of independent gangs that adopt a similar

* E-mail address: ykchu@hkucc.hku.hk

organizational structure and ritual to bind their members together. Although various societies are symbolically part of the triad 'family', they are decentralized in that no one central body is able to unite all triad societies, or to give universal commands. The triads' organizational structure has become flexible and decentralized. The traditional rank system has been largely reduced to three – Red Pole, 49 and Blue Lanterns. The initiation ceremony has been simplified. Most people joined a triad society based on an oral agreement with their Big Brother. Traditionally San Yee On triad society liked to conduct the full initiation ceremony for their newly recruited members. However, in the last few years we seldom heard about that San Yee On arranged the elaborate initiation ceremony for their new members.

Today it is no longer possible for many triad societies to enforce strict discipline over their members. Membership transfer can be done quite easily. Triad Big Brothers have no obligation to look after their followers who encounter problems. Compared with other triad groups, the senior members of the San Yee On triad society are relatively coherent. They may offer assistance to each other, especially when their members are in legal troubles.

It is evident that San Yee On members are found in USA, Canada, UK and Australia. In USA some individual members may have connections with the Fuk Ching Gangs. However, it should be noted that this is not an organized movement launched by San Yee On in Hong Kong. No mass triad migration to Western counties has ever happened before nor has it happened after 1997. Their connections with overseas criminal organizations are largely based on personal networks and probably there is nothing to do with the Society.

3. Violence

In Hong Kong young triad Big Brothers may use violence to establish their reputation in the community. Individual triad members may be more violent than others. However different triad groups tend to use 'settlement talk' to solve their disputes. Although triad bosses may mobilize a large number of their followers or hire other gangsters to demonstrate their power in the settlement talk meeting, serious mass triad gang fight cases were not found in Hong Kong in the last few years.

Firearms are tightly controlled by the Hong Kong government. Triad members seldom use firearms to kill. According to police records, few homicide cases were done by triads. In Hong Kong we cannot find any cases that police officers or government officials were killed by triads because of their job duties in the last few years.

4. Economic Resources

Individual San Yee On members may get involved in drugs, pirated VCD/DVD trade in the street, speculative activities in the stock market, money laundering, vehicle theft and smuggling, prostitution, extortion, loan sharking, illegal gambling and so on, but they are not required to get permission from the Society to conduct these businesses. In fact these are personal investments and individual members will not transfer part of their profits to the Society.

In the past San Yee On members were known to be active in international drug trafficking, especially importing heroin from Thailand to Hong Kong and some of the drugs were smuggled to Western countries. Although individual San Yee On members are still doing the drug business, we have no sufficient evidence to support that San Yee On members play a significant role in the trade. In fact, other triad members and the people without triad members can get involved in the business if they have the capital, connections and skills to do it.

Although indicators have showed that individual San Yee On members may have been involved in some specific legitimate business such as catering businesses, the film industry or even in the stock market, their roles in the legitimate economy are not certain. For instance, it is difficult to confirm whether they are simply legal entrepreneurs, using their triad reputation to monopolize the business, or laundering their money through investing legitimate business. Compared with other triad groups, it is quite clear that San Yee On members have intended to participate in more non-violent crime such as black market crime and economic crime. In addition, they have more connections with legitimate business entrepreneurs and professionals like lawyers and accountants.

5. Political Resources

Hong Kong has a clean civil service. The criminal justice professionals are well paid. The system to monitor the proper functioning of the legal procedure is well established. The Independent Commission Against Corruption (ICAC) is a powerful law enforcement agency to combat corruption. There are no indicators that large-scale corruption syndicates exist within the Hong Kong criminal justice system.

Hong Kong triads are not interested in involving themselves in politics. We cannot see any triad group that is able to manipulate politicians and the political process in Hong Kong and abroad. There is also no evidence to support that triads have managed to get their members elected to the Legislature. Before 1997, some journalists reported that senior San Yee On members were connected to high-ranking Chinese government officials. But in the last few years, we seldom heard about this kind of reports.

6. Response of Law Enforcement Agencies to Organized Crime

In the last few years the Hong Kong Police tried to focus on targeting the source of triad criminal income. Therefore, a number of operations were launched to combat their vice and illegal gambling activities. The Hong Kong Police also sent undercover agents to penetrate different triad societies to collect intelligence about their criminal activities. In addition, financial investigation techniques were regularly employed to trace and then confiscate their criminal proceeds. The Hong Kong Police also maintain close liaison and cooperation with different law enforcement agencies in the Mainland China, Macau and overseas in order to combat cross-border and transnational triad activities. In his 2004 Operational Targets, the Commissioner of Police summarized the following measures to fight against triad-related activities:

- Strengthen the Force intelligence network and enhance cooperation amongst units at all levels;
- Enhance professionalism in the response to and investigation of triad-related incidents;
- Continue to mount strategic undercover operations;
- Proactively target key triad personalities and activities;
- Optimize the use of the Organized and Serious Crimes Ordinance in investigating triad related cases;
- Continue to exchange intelligence with the Mainland and Macau authorities as well as overseas law enforcement agencies.

Compared with other social issues in Hong Kong, the priority about triads and their organized crime activities is always high on the public agenda especially due to grave concern about the occurrence of some collective violent cases. It should nevertheless be noted that triad activities have nothing to do with the everyday life of most Hong Kong people. Local people strongly believe that Hong Kong is a very safe city. People perceived triads as a menace because they are portrayed as such in the sensational media reports and gang movies. For ordinary Hong Kong people, their most concern about triads may not be their organized crime activities, but their influences on the vulnerable juvenile, especially the so-called 'triad infiltration to schools'.

Wo Shing Wo

1. Background

According to police records, only 14 out of the 50 triad societies remain active in Hong Kong. Out of these 14 active groups, Wo Shing Wo is regarded as one of the most influential triad groups. Wo Shing Wo was originally an off-shoot society of Wo Hop To which was established in 1908. Wo Shing Wo broke away from Wo Hop To in 1930 and then became an independent triad society. Members of Wo Shing Wo come from different walks of life. A small number of local born Indian and Pakistan are also recruited to the Society. Nevertheless, Wo Shing Wo is still a male dominant secret society. Few females joined the Society formally.

2. Organizational Structure

It is true that triad societies are secret organizations, but they are in fact loose cartels consisting of a number of independent gangs that adopt a similar organizational structure and ritual to bind their members together. Although various societies are symbolically part of the triad 'family', they are decentralized in that no one central body is able to unite all triad societies, or to give universal commands. The triads' organizational structure has become flexible and decentralized. The traditional rank system has been largely reduced to three – Red Pole, 49 and Blue Lanterns. The initiation ceremony has been simplified. Most people joined a triad society based on an oral agreement with their Big Brother. Today it is no longer possible for many triad societies to enforce strict discipline over their members. Membership transfer can be done quite easily. Triad Big Brothers have no obligation to look after their followers who encounter problems.

Wo Shing Wo has a Central Committee composed of a body of influential and senior officials. The Chairman and Treasurer now known locally as Cho Kun and Cha So, are often elected form this body at an annual or bi-annual meeting. The leadership in the Central Committee may help to settle internal and external disputes but they are unable to dictate to their members in which criminal activities they should get involved.

It is evident that Wo Shing Wo members are found in UK, Canada and USA. According to police sources, some individual members may have connections with the Big Circle Gangs in Holland. However, it should be noted that their connections with overseas criminal organizations are largely based on personal networks and probably there is nothing to do with the Society. There are no indicates that mass Wo Shing Wo triad migration to Western counties has ever happened before nor has it happened after 1997.

3. Violence

In Hong Kong young triad Big Brothers may use violence to establish their reputation in the community. Individual triad members may be more violent than others. However different triad groups tend to use 'settlement talk' to solve their disputes. Although triad bosses may mobilize a large number of their followers or hire other gangsters to demonstrate their power in the settlement talk meeting, serious mass triad gang fight cases were not found in Hong Kong in the last few years.

Firearms are tightly controlled by the Hong Kong government. Triad members seldom use firearms to kill. According to police records, few homicide cases were done by triads. In Hong Kong we cannot find any cases that police officers or government officials were killed by triads because of their job duties in the last few years.

4. Economic Resources

Individual Wo Shing Wo members may get involved in drugs, pirated VCD/DVD trade in the street, London Gold scams, money laundering, vehicle theft and smuggling, prostitution, extortion, loan sharking, illegal gambling and so on, but they are not required to get permission from the Society to conduct these businesses. In fact these are personal investments and individual members will not transfer part of their profits to the Society. According to police sources, Wo Shing Wo members have their strength in the pirated

VCD/DVD industry. They not only get involved in street-level distribution but also the manufacturing of pirated VCD/DVDs. Compared with other triad groups, Wo Shing Wo members intended to participate in more violent crime and tried to be dominant in the street-level organized crime in the last few years.

Although indicators have showed that individual Wo Shing Wo members have been involved in some specific legitimate businesses such as catering and entertainment business, their roles in the legitimate economy are not certain. For instance, it is difficult to confirm whether they are simply legal entrepreneurs, using their triad reputation to monopolize the business, or laundering their money through investing legitimate business.

5. Political Resources

Hong Kong has a clean civil service. The criminal justice professionals are well paid. The system to monitor the proper functioning of the legal procedure is well established. The Independent Commission Against Corruption (ICAC) is a powerful law enforcement agency to combat corruption. There are no indicators that large-scale corruption syndicates exist within the Hong Kong criminal justice system.

Hong Kong triads are not interested in involving themselves in politics. We cannot see any triad group that is able to manipulate politicians and the political process in Hong Kong and abroad. There is also no evidence to support that triads have managed to get their members elected to the Legislature.

6. Response of Law Enforcement Agencies to Organized Crime

In the last few years the Hong Kong Police tried to focus on targeting the source of triad criminal income. Therefore, a number of operations were launched to combat their vice and illegal gambling activities. The Hong Kong Police also sent undercover agents to penetrate different triad societies to collect intelligence about their criminal activities. In addition, financial investigation techniques were regularly employed to trace and then confiscate their criminal proceeds. The Hong Kong Police also maintain close liaison and cooperation with different law enforcement agencies in the Mainland China, Macau and overseas in order to combat cross-border and transnational triad activities. In his 2004 Operational Targets, the Commissioner of Police summarized the following measures to fight against triad-related activities:

- Strengthen the Force intelligence network and enhance cooperation amongst units at all levels;
- Enhance professionalism in the response to and investigation of triad-related incidents;
- Continue to mount strategic undercover operations;
- Proactively target key triad personalities and activities;
- Optimize the use of the Organized and Serious Crimes Ordinance in investigating triad related cases;
- Continue to exchange intelligence with the Mainland and Macau authorities as well as overseas law enforcement agencies.

7. The External Environment

Compared with other social issues in Hong Kong, the priority about triads and their organized crime activities is always high on the public agenda especially due to grave concern about the occurrence of some collective violent cases. It should nevertheless be noted that triad activities have nothing to do with the everyday life of most Hong Kong people. Local people strongly believe that Hong Kong is a very safe city. People perceived triads as a menace because they are portrayed as such in the sensational media reports and gang movies. For ordinary Hong Kong people, their most concern about triads may not be their organized crime activities, but their influences on the vulnerable juvenile, especially the so-called ‘triad infiltration to schools’.

14K

1. Background

According to police records, only 14 out of the 50 triad societies remain active in Hong Kong. Out of these 14 active groups, 14K is regarded as one of the most influential triad groups. 14K was formed in Hong Kong in the early 1950s by a group of triad members with the Nationalist Party background in Guangdong province. Nowadays members of 14K come from different walks of life. A small number of local born Indian and Pakistan are also recruited to the Society. Nevertheless, 14K is still a male dominant secret society. Few females joined the Society formally.

2. Organizational Structure

It is true that triad societies are secret organizations, but they are in fact loose cartels consisting of a number of independent gangs that adopt a similar organizational structure and ritual to bind their members together. Although various societies are symbolically part of the triad 'family', they are decentralized in that no one central body is able to unite all triad societies, or to give universal commands. The triads' organizational structure has become flexible and decentralized. The traditional rank system has been largely reduced to three – Red Pole, 49 and Blue Lanterns. The initiation ceremony has been simplified. Most people joined a triad society based on an oral agreement with their Big Brother. Today it is no longer possible for many triad societies to enforce strict discipline over their members. Membership transfer can be done quite easily. Triad Big Brothers have no obligation to look after their followers who encounter problems.

Compared with other triad groups, 14K is relatively disorganized. It has different sub-groups and they have developed into separate triad societies in their own right. Gang fights among different sub-groups are not uncommon. It is evident that 14K members are found in UK, Holland, USA, Canada and Australia. According to police sources, some individual members may have connections with the Big Circle Gangs in Holland, Yakuza in Japan and the United Bamboo Gangs in Taiwan. However, it should be noted that their connections with overseas criminal organizations are largely based on personal networks and probably there is nothing to do with the Society. There are no indicates that mass 14K triad migration to Western counties has ever happened before nor has it happened after 1997.

3. Violence

In Hong Kong young triad Big Brothers may use violence to establish their reputation in the community. Individual triad members may be more violent than others. However different triad groups tend to use 'settlement talk' to solve their disputes. Although triad bosses may mobilize a large number of their followers or hire other gangsters to demonstrate their power in the settlement talk meeting, serious mass triad gang fight cases were not found in Hong Kong in the last few years.

Firearms are tightly controlled by the Hong Kong government. Triad members seldom use firearms to kill. According to police records, few homicide cases were done by triads. In Hong Kong we cannot find any cases that police officers or government officials were killed by triads because of their job duties in the last few years.

4. Economic Resources

Individual 14K members may get involved in drugs, pirated VCD/DVD trade in the street, London Gold scams, money laundering, vehicle theft and smuggling, prostitution, extortion, loan sharking, illegal gambling and so on, but they are not required to get permission from the Society to conduct these businesses. In fact these are personal investments and individual members will not transfer part of their profits to the Society. According to police sources, 14K members have their strength in organizing illegal gambling including underground casinos and illegal bookmaking. In addition, many detected London Gold scams showed that 14K members were the organizers and operators. Compared with other triad groups, 14K members tend to continue to participate in their traditional street-level organized crime.

Although indicators have showed that individual 14K members have been involved in some specific legitimate businesses such as catering and entertainment businesses, their roles in the legitimate economy are not certain. For instance, it is difficult to confirm whether they are simply legal entrepreneurs, using their triad reputation to monopolize the business, or laundering their money through investing legitimate businesses.

5. Political Resources

Hong Kong has a clean civil service. The criminal justice professionals are well paid. The system to monitor the proper functioning of the legal procedure is well established. The Independent Commission Against Corruption (ICAC) is a powerful law enforcement agency to combat corruption. There are no indicators that large-scale corruption syndicates exist within the Hong Kong criminal justice system.

Hong Kong triads are not interested in involving themselves in politics. We cannot see any triad group that is able to manipulate politicians and the political process in Hong Kong and abroad. There is also no evidence to support that triads have managed to get their members elected to the Legislature.

14K was formed in Hong Kong in the early 1950s by a group of triad members with the Nationalist Party background in Guangdong province. It is true that some 14K members had a close relationship with senior Nationalist Party members in Taiwan in 1960s and 1970s. Nowadays, we cannot see that 14K members are interested in political movements.

6. Response of Law Enforcement Agencies to Organized Crime

In the last few years the Hong Kong Police tried to focus on targeting the source of triad criminal income. Therefore, a number of operations were launched to combat their vice and illegal gambling activities. The Hong Kong Police also sent undercover agents to penetrate different triad societies to collect intelligence about their criminal activities. In addition, financial investigation techniques were regularly employed to trace and then confiscate their criminal proceeds. The Hong Kong Police also maintain close liaison and cooperation with different law enforcement agencies in the Mainland China, Macau and overseas in order to combat cross-border and transnational triad activities. In his 2004 Operational Targets, the Commissioner of Police summarized the following measures to fight against triad-related activities:

- Strengthen the Force intelligence network and enhance cooperation amongst units at all levels;
- Enhance professionalism in the response to and investigation of triad-related incidents;
- Continue to mount strategic undercover operations;
- Proactively target key triad personalities and activities;
- Optimize the use of the Organized and Serious Crimes Ordinance in investigating triad related cases;
- Continue to exchange intelligence with the Mainland and Macau authorities as well as overseas law enforcement agencies.

7. The External Environment

Compared with other social issues in Hong Kong, the priority about triads and their organized crime activities is always high on the public agenda especially due to grave concern about the occurrence of some collective violent cases. It should nevertheless be noted that triad activities have nothing to do with the everyday life of most Hong Kong people. Local people strongly believe that Hong Kong is a very safe city. People perceived triads as a menace because they are portrayed as such in the sensational media reports and gang movies. For ordinary Hong Kong people, their most concern about triads may not be their organized crime activities, but their influences on the vulnerable juvenile, especially the so-called 'triad infiltration to schools'.

REFERENCES

Chu, Y.K. (2002) Global Triads: Myth or Reality? In Berdal, M.R, and Serrano, M. (ed.) *Transnational Organized Crime and International Security: Business As Usual*. Pp. 183-193. Boulder Colo.: Lynne Rienner.

Chu, Y.K. (2000) The Triads As Business. London and New York: Routledge.

In: Organized Crime, Gangs and Trafficking ISBN: 978-1-61122-829-8
Editors: C. Webb and P. Dobrev

Chapter 7

THE TRAFFICKING OF MAINLAND CHINESE WOMEN TO TAIWAN FOR THE PURPOSE OF PROSTITUTION

James O. Finckenauer and Ko-Lin Chin

I. INTRODUCTION

According to statistical data released on March 31, 2004 by the National Police Administration (NPA), 2,345 illegal immigrants from China were arrested in the year 2003. The number of arrested illegal immigrants has increased by 28% (512) over 2002. Among the arrestees, 1,001 people (43%) said they were not employed yet at the time of their arrests, 894 people (38%) admitted they were working as prostitutes, and 418 people (18%) said they were illegally employed. In 2003, it was the first time that illegal female immigrants (1,962) outnumbered illegal male immigrants, a result of a 41% (569) increase from the previous year. Among the female immigrants, 894 said they were sex workers, 840 indicated they were not yet employed. Among female immigrants, 1,233 (36%) were between the age of 16 and 20, which is the largest age group. There were 1,095 (32%) women between the age of 21 and 25, which is the second largest age group. There were 521 (15%) women between the age of 26 to 30, which is the third largest age group. In sum, most illegal immigrants from China were young females.

The majority of the illegal immigrants were arrested in three different areas: the coastal area, inland, and on the sea. Over the years, most illegal immigrants were arrested inland. In inland areas, 2,603 people were arrested in 2003, an increase of 44% (797) from 2002. Among them, police arrested 1,845 (71%) people, mostly in Taipei City, Taipei County, Taoyuan County and Taichung City. There were 754 (29%) illegal immigrants arrested by the Coast Guard Administration. Three hundred and fifty illegal immigrants were arrested on the water in 2003, a decrease of 27% (127) from the previous year. All of those were apprehended by officers from the Coast Guard Administration. On March 31, 2004, there were 2,155 illegal immigrants being detained in various detention centers exclusively for Mainland Chinese. Among them 1,132 people were detained in the center in Yilan, 1,011 people in the center in Hsinchu, and 12 people in the center in Matsu.

II. Channels for Mainland Chinese Women to Travel to Taiwan

A Brief Introduction

There are three ways for Chinese women to come to Taiwan: "marriage," "visit," and smuggling. Because rules for visiting relatives are very strict, it is difficult for Chinese to obtain a visa to visit their relatives in Taiwan. Therefore, mainland Chinese sex workers in Taiwan rarely enter the country utilizing this method. The most common channels for those women who are willing to work in the sex industry in Taiwan is to arrive in Taiwan by using "fake marriage" and smuggling. Usually, people in a fake marriage enter Taiwan through international airports (so they are called "air force" in jargon). Smuggled people enter Taiwan usually by fishing boats (so they are called "navy" in jargon). Since it is hard to obtain travel documents to enter Taiwan by air, rarely do Chinese being smuggled into Taiwan come by air.

Going to Taiwan through Fake Marriage

The reasons for Chinese women to come to Taiwan through fake marriage are (1) lack of job opportunities and (2) low income in China. Usually they are introduced by friends or recruited by human traffickers.

A man is chosen to be the fake husband. Usually, fake husbands are recruited by human trafficking groups in Taiwan. Some of them are wanderers, and most of them are people with lower class backgrounds with little financial resources and are tempted by the extra-income of being a fake husband. According to data from the Aviation Police Bureau of the National Police Administration, fewer and fewer Chinese women were coming to Taiwan this way in the past year due to police crackdowns.

At the beginning of the process, a human trafficking group will arrange a fake husband to travel to China. He will bring along his single certificate to China so that he can file a marriage registration with a woman in China (for trafficking purposes, being registered with the Chinese authorities is good enough. As a result, fake marriage is different from a genuine marriage in which conducting an elaborate wedding ceremony is a must. Thus, whether a couple conducted a wedding ceremony or not is a good way to differentiate the fake from the real marriage). After a marriage is registered, under current laws a newlywed bride is entitled to apply for a visa to visit her husband in Taiwan. According to the Statute Governing Relations Between People of the Taiwan Area and the Mainland Area, a spouse from China can stay in Taiwan for a month per visit, and if she passes an interview with Taiwanese authorities, she can extend her stay for five more months. If she applies to go to Taiwan again, she can get a visa for six months to stay in Taiwan. In other words, a sex worker who arrives in Taiwan through fake marriage can stay in Taiwan for a maximum of six months per visit (the old regulations, revised on January 2004, allowed a Chinese spouse to stay in Taiwan for three months and apply for an extension for another three months). Based on interview information from Chinese sex workers, normally a Chinese sex worker can earn a relatively large amount of money during the six months stay in Taiwan. After her visa has expired, she returns to China, then divorces her fake husband immediately. It has also been found that, in some cases, before fake wives come to Taiwan, they had an agreement with their fake husbands that they will go to Taiwan twice for a total of twelve months stay. For a sex worker staying in Taiwan for twelve months, the only relationship between her and her fake husband is monetary: she has to pay her fake husband NT$30,000 per month [about $900] and the fake husband must accompany her when she goes for an interview with the authorities for extending her stay. Her living arrangement is set up by a human trafficking group. They will also assign a driver to drive her to work.

Going to Taiwan by Boat

Clandestine immigration is called jor tongji or riding a bucket [bucket means boat in Taiwanese]. This method is simpler than fake marriage. First, human smuggling groups seek suitable women who are willing to work in Taiwan. Some women may initiate the contacts with human trafficking groups in the hope that they can go to Taiwan to make money. Then, these women will be smuggled by human traffickers to Taiwan. Most departing locations are in the coastal areas of Fujian Province. For the purpose of smuggling more people, they are compelled to throw away their luggage. They are carried by mainland Chinese fishing boats (called "mainland horses" in jargon) to the sea. In certain locations in the Taiwan Strait, they are transferred to Taiwanese fishing boats (called "Taiwanese horses" in jargon). Human smuggling groups will pay NT$ 70,000-NT$100,000 [$2,100 to $3,000] to the fishing boat owner for every smuggled woman (In January 2003, the price rose to NT$150,000-NT$200,000 [$4,500 to $6,000]).

While changing boats, because of bad weather and strong waves, women will be thrown between the boats like goods in order to speed up the transfer. During an interview, a woman said her ears and hearing were damaged because of this. As to the landing locations in Taiwan, these women have no knowledge. After landing in Taiwan, they are sent to hidden places, and then they are sold in auctions arranged by human trafficking groups. People from the sex industry are invited to the auctions. Agents within the commercial sex community are the bidders. The price to buy a woman from the auction usually is around NT$120,000 – NT$200,000 [$3,600 to $6,000]. Then the woman who has been sold will be transferred to a place near where she is going to work. Agents will take these women with them to visit sex brokers (pimps or, in Taiwanese, "cats." Also called auntie, internal general, or chicken head). After a customer contacts a chicken head, the latter will get in touch with an agent to "deploy" a sex worker. The agent will send the girl to a designated place. At the beginning stage, when a sex worker from mainland China starts working, persons from human trafficking group supervise her work. After a while, she will be taken care by a designated "jockey" or driver.

III. Modus Operandi of Commercial Sex Organizations

A General Description

Regardless of how Chinese women are smuggled to Taiwan, their methods of payment vary. Only a very small number of them either pay their smugglers the entire fee up front or pay a down payment before departure and pay off the balance in China after arriving in Taiwan. For the majority of the women, they do not pay any fees. Instead, various sex ring organizations will front the money. After the women arrive in Taiwan, they will go to work and repay their smuggling fees from their income.

Operational Patterns

Taiwan as a whole is divided into Northern Area (Taipei area), Central Area (Taichung area), and Southern Area (Kaohsiung Area) and other smaller areas such as Taoyuan, Hsinchu, and Tainan. As far as the sex business is concerned, every area is unique.

In the Taipei Area, operational patterns involving mainland Chinese sex workers could be categorized into three: (1) "take out," "fixed location" and "one apartment one phoenix."

Take Out

Under this pattern, a customer will check into a hotel, get in touch with a pimp, and a sex worker will be delivered to the customer's room. The price for "taking out" is about 2.5K to 4K ("K" is a slang used by people in the commercial sex world to indicate the amount of money. 1K is NT$1,000 [about $30]. One "volume" means NT$100,000 [$3,000]). Sex ring operators often categorize sex workers into "high class" and "low class." High-class sex workers are further categorized based on their sophistication, and each category signifies a different NT$1,000 amount. Currently, the highest price for Mainland Chinese prostitutes in the Taipei area is 8K. All prostitutes in the Taipei area, regardless of their nationalities, are categorized into these various "classes." Another method to find a mainland Chinese sex worker is to check into a hotel and ask an "internal general" (a hotel employee who is also often called "auntie") to find a sex worker. This "internal general" is essentially a pimp, while being a full-time employee of a hotel. Under such circumstances, the on-going price is between 3K to 5K and more often than not, the sex worker is from China. However, not all hotels in the Taipei area have this type of extra service. It depends on the state of mind of the owner of a hotel and the willingness of its employees to play the additional role as a pimp.

Fixed Location

A fixed location is also called a "chicken den." In the Taiwanese dialect, it is called a "private brothel." Most sex workers in these chicken dens are from China. These chicken dens are very similar to the traditional Taiwanese brothels called "dried tofu," so named because these brothels are haphazardly built by metal sheets and congregated in a certain area. From a bird's eye view, these brothels are like dried tofu stacked against one another. Dried tofu brothels are mostly staffed by Taiwanese sex workers, the time for a sex transaction is limited (about 15 minutes per trick), and the environment is far from ideal (a small room partitioned with wood panels). Currently, these dried tofu brothels are mostly located in Keelung, San Chung City (Taipei County), Chungli (Taoyuan County), and Hsinchu. Chicken dens staffed predominantly with mainland Chinese cost about 2.5K—3K per visit. A chicken den owner will rent a house or an apartment in a residential area and make it looks like an ordinary dwelling place. A chicken den owner will rent a house or an apartment with at least three rooms. For the safety of the sex workers and customers, the sexual services are provided in the rooms of the chicken den; no girls will be allowed to leave the premises with a customer. Those working in the chicken dens are mostly smuggled into Taiwan from China by boats, and they are often moved from one chicken den to another. In addition, to evade law enforcement authorities, a customer would have access to these places only through someone who had been there before.

One Studio One Phoenix

The One Studio One Phoenix mode of operations is most prevalent in Taipei City and fixed locations are mostly located in Taipei County. Most studios are located in an apartment complex. When a customer gets to the complex, the chicken head will tell the customer a room number to go to. After the customer ring the bell, a sex worker will open the door. If the customer does not like what he sees, he will get in touch with the chicken head downstairs and a new room number will be offered. These places often restrict the transaction to one hour, but some places do not set time limits, as long as a sex worker does not have another customer waiting. These One Studio One Phoenix operations involve both "Taiwanese Tea" (Taiwanese women) and "Water Tea" (Mainland Chinese women). Some studios are famous for the quality of their service, and some are appealing because they are staffed predominantly with Mainland Chinese women. Taiwanese sex workers in these studios include both full-time and part-time workers. Mainland Chinese working in these establishments may come to Taiwan on their own or by being smuggled into Taiwan by sex ring operators. A sex worker could be bought by a chicken head for an entire day and he will put her in a rented studio and go out to recruit customers. The quality and the age of the women in the studios can be widely varied. The fee for a visit to a studio is between 2.8K to 3.5K. As with the fixed locations, these studios can be found only with the help of an old customer. The One Studio One Phoenix mode of sex operation was originated in Hong Kong and it became popular in Taipei in the past ten years. In Taipei, the studios were initially the dwelling places of bar girls where they entertained their best customers or their lovers. Gradually, these places were transformed into One Studio One Phoenix operations. Consequently, most of these studios are now situated near the red light districts where a large number of studio apartments are located. Chicken heads can be seen at night wandering around these complexes in their attempts to recruit customers.

In the Taichung area, the most prevalent mode of operation is the "take out." However, sex workers there are rarely delivered to hotels, but if so, it is mostly to five-star hotels. The "take out" operation in the Taichung area often work like this: A chicken head will rent a three-story residential property and then convert the first floor into a lobby. After a customer arrives, the chicken head will contact a sex ring operator and ask for mainland Chinese women. After a customer picks a girl he likes, the two will go upstairs. The price is about 2.5K for ordinary sex workers. For high class women, the price is 3K and above. However, there are not many high class sex workers in Taichung.

In Kaohsiung, the most prevalent mode of operation is similar to the "take out" operation in Taipei. Fixed location and One Studio One Phoenix modes of operation are almost nonexistent in the area. The price for "lower class" sex workers in Kaohsiung is 2K per date, and 2.5K for "higher class." Some hotels in Kaohsiung will, to attract more business, provide a free room if a customer asks for sex service. According to fieldwork conducted in May 2004, there were about 500 Mainland Chinese working in the area at the end of 2003 and the sex business is dominated by four to six upper-level [large] organizations. However, due to recent police crackdowns, there are currently only 200 mainland Chinese sex workers. The uniqueness of the sex trade in Kaohsiung is that the operators there are relatively unified and better organized.

IV. The Distribution of Income within a Sex Ring

In the Taipei area, a sex worker from Mainland China charges about NT$3,000 [$90] per trick (due to recent police crackdowns, the price has recently increased to NT$3,500 [$105]). Of course, this number is just a rough estimate, because the price may vary significantly based on a sex worker's attractiveness and service. For each date, a mainland Chinese sex worker will receive NT$1,100 – 1,500 [from $33 to $45] and the rest will go to the sex ring operator. The mode is to pay a sex worker 40% of the income and the sex ring operator 60%. According to an interview conducted in Taipei with a sex ring operator around April 2004, if a chicken head (or pimp) charges a customer NT$3,000, he or she will turn over NT$2,200 (NT$3,000 x 0.8 – NT$200) to the "company" (the sex ring organization). The "company" will pay the "agent" (the agent of the sex worker or the "owner" who had bought the woman in an auction) NT$1,800 (NT$3,000 x 0.6). Of this, the agent will give the sex worker NT$1,200. If a sex worker has already repaid her smuggling fees, she will be offered more money per trick as a bonus from the "owner."

A sex worker will clear the book with her "owner" every 7 to 10 days. Her "owner" will then help her to wire the money to China via the underground banking system or gold stores. An "owner" may also wire the money from a bank in Hong Kong into the sex workers' bank account in China. A mainland Chinese woman is responsible for her daily expenses and rent. Besides, a sex worker has to pay her "jockey" or car driver NT$3,000 [$90] a day and her "fake husband" NT$30,000 [$900] a month, and to repay the "owner" for the amount of money he spent to buy her in an auction. In general, a mainland Chinese sex worker must perform about 200 tricks to clear her debt and begin to have her own "real income" because income from the first 200 dates would have to be used to cover her daily expenses, rent, driver, fake husband, and smuggling debt. If a sex worker performs 6 to 8 tricks on an average per day, it is estimated that she would have had 200 tricks in a month. That's why if a sex worker is not arrested by the police within a month of her arrival, the agent who bought her is guaranteed a profit.

V. Jockey: A Unique Role in the Sex Business

The "jockey" (driver) is the bridge between a sex worker and a sex ring. Normally, one jockey will be assigned to one girl. In the past, a jockey is most likely to drive a sex worker around in a yellow taxi, but because of recent crackdowns, more and more jockeys are switching to private, unmarked cars. A driver will drive a sex worker around to the customers because most mainland Chinese women are not familiar with their new environment. Whenever a customer contacts a sex ring (normally the chicken head), the chicken head will select a sex ring after he or she listened to the special needs of the customer. An operator of the sex ring will then instruct a jockey to drive a sex worker to the customer's place. While the sex worker is with the customer, the driver will park his car around the vicinity to keep an eye on the people going in and out of the hotel and to keep track of the time. Ten minutes before the time is up, he will call the sex worker to hurry up. Of course, if the driver observes some law enforcement personnel, he will also alert her and the customer. When the sex worker comes out of the hotel with the money collected from the customer, she will immediately hand it over to the driver to avoid being robbed by a subsequent customer. At the end of the day, the driver will turn over all the day's earnings to the sex ring. When the sex worker is not with a customer, the driver will keep an eye on her and wait for instructions from the sex ring. The driver is also responsible for making sure the sex worker is not deprived of food. While waiting for business, the driver and the sex worker may find a secure place to rest and wait or drive around a certain area or go shopping. When a sex worker is off due to menstruation, the driver may take a short break. However, it is also reported that the driver may have to go shopping with the sex worker during this period. From the sex worker's perspective, a driver may also be a guardian. The driver is also responsible for another important function. That is, whenever an agent buys a new girl and the girl is packaged accordingly, the driver will drive the new girl to various chicken heads to be examined or "interviewed" in the hope that these chicken heads will be familiar with the newly arrived sex worker and bring business to her. In a sense, for most Mainland Chinese sex workers in Taiwan, the one person with whom she is most familiar is her jockey.

VI. Going Home

The dream of mainland Chinese sex workers in Taiwan is to make a certain amount of money and then return home. Because they do not have legal status in Taiwan, they can not settle down in Taiwan, and the best they can do is to go home on a good note. However, due to police crackdowns, many of them are deported back to China.

If the Taiwanese police arrest a sex worker from China, the authorities will, according to the Kinmen Agreement between China and Taiwan, first check the arrestees' background to make sure she is a Chinese citizen and then inform the Chinese authorities. While waiting for the Chinese government to take her back, she will be kept in a "Mainland Chinese Processing Center," the so-called Jinru center. In Taiwan, there are currently two detention centers for illegal mainland Chinese, one in Hsinchu and one in Yilan. In the past, to solve the problem of overcrowding at the two detention centers, local police bureaus and the Coast Guard Administration converted some of their cells into temporary holding pens for Chinese sex workers. However, because it is too problematic to detain illegal female migrants in these facilities and because it is a drain on the police, the majority of them are now kept in the Jinru centers. Those who come to Taiwan via fake marriages are by law required to buy a roundtrip air ticket and, as a result, they will be immediately asked to fly back to China after being briefly detained.

There is little information on the return trip of mainland Chinese women who are never arrested by Taiwanese authorities. In May 2004, however, authorities in northern Taiwan discovered nine mainland Chinese women who were about to board a boat. According to the authorities, the nine women were all dressed fashionably and they all seemed to have been in Taiwan for a period of time. Because the case is still under investigation, all the details are still not known. However, from interviews with sex ring operators, people who are in the smuggling business will once in a while contact sex establishment owners to find out whether there are Chinese sex workers who would like to return home. If there are such women, the smugglers will transport these women – usually about 10 in group – out of Taiwan right after they bring in a group of women from China into Taiwan. The patterns and the routes of the two processes are the same, it is just that one group comes in and one group goes out. Each returnee is reported to have to pay between NT$80,000 to NT$100,000 [$2,400 to $3,000] for the trip home.

In: Organized Crime, Gangs and Trafficking ISBN: 978-1-61122-829-8
Editors: C. Webb and P. Dobrev

Chapter 8

HONG KONG DRUG TRAFFICKING SITUATION–2003 (WITH 2004 UPDATE)

James O. Finckenauer and Ko-Lin Chin

TRENDS AND SEIZURES

In 2003, a high priority was again accorded to tackling psychotropic substance abuse. Police were able to consolidate on the success in the previous year in reducing the problem. When compared to 2002 there was a 25% decrease in the number of young persons arrested in respect of psychotropic substance cases. Throughout the year police made every effort to cut-off the supply of psychotropic substances to the mainly young abusers. During numerous enforcement operations, various police units joined forces to enhance the effectiveness in quelling the psychotropic substance problem.

The heroin reaching the Hong Kong, Special Administrative Region (SAR) invariably originates from the Golden Triangle. The heroin is smuggled overland through Mainland China to clandestine stores in areas of southern China adjacent to the SAR. Hong Kong syndicates arrange for numerous small amounts of heroin to be smuggled into Hong Kong via the land boundary with the Mainland. The sheer volume of traffic coming through the boundary provides opportunities for traffickers to avoid detection. As Hong Kong is not used as a significant drug transit centre nowadays, heroin smuggled into the SAR is for local abusers. At the start of the year heroin divans (premises where addicts go to purchase and consume the narcotic) were a major focus of attention for police. The majority were situated in the Kowloon West Region. Numerous operations to neutralize the divans resulted in a substantial reduction in such premises operating towards the end of the year.

Three heroin-cutting centres were dismantled in 2003. Arrests in relation to heroin offences were down by around 5.2% when compared to the previous year. A total of 52.87 KGs kilograms of heroin were seized.

The average wholesale price of heroin in 2003 was HK$256,638 per kilogram, an increase when compared to the average wholesale price HK$222,592 in 2002. The average retail price of heroin increased from HK$419.91 per gram in 2002 to HK$424.75 per gram in 2003. Retail purity increased to an average of 59% when compared to an average purity of 41.5% in 2002.

Ketamine seizures and arrests were again relatively high in 2003. The drug has now become firmly established as the most prevalent drug of abuse among young persons in the SAR. The abuse of ketamine was inextricably linked to the still popular rave/dance party music scene in the SAR. With a diminishing number of dance parties held in large hired venues, abuse tended to be in discos, bars, karaoke lounges or in private settings. The number of persons arrested for offences related to ketamine in 2003 was 1,770, a fall of 24.9% on the preceding year. In 2003, the average wholesale price of ketamine was HK$57,125 per kilogram and the average retail price was HK$194 per gram.

Again in 2003, as seen in recent years, there were tablets in circulation, being sold to consumers as "ecstasy", that were found to contain a mixture of dangerous drugs. Many tablets seized contained a mix of ketamine and methamphetamine. Those tablets that contained MDMA, the substance originally associated with the term ecstasy, were found to contain a wide variation in the volume of the active ingredient. In some tablets the MDMA content was as low as 70 mg, in others it was more than double at around 150 mg per tablet. Ecstasy-type tablets are brought into Hong Kong from production sources by couriers. Packages of the small (roughly 8mm diameter) tablets are taped to the body and hidden under clothing or concealed in luggage. The retail price of an ecstasy-type tablet decreased from around HK$90 in 2002 to around HK$85 in 2003. Over the year, a total of 141,038 ecstasy-type tablets were seized, an almost three-fold increase when compared with 48,840 tablets seized in 2002. The increase can be ascribed to three major cases where several thousands of tablets were seized. In a significant case, a fairly sophisticated ecstasy-type tablet production enterprise based in Kowloon was dismantled.

Passengers concealing small quantities on their person or in luggage bring cannabis from the Golden Triangle and Cambodia into the SAR. Larger consignments may be smuggled by the sea route. The total herbal cannabis seizures for the year amounted to 586.61 kilograms. The average wholesale price of herbal cannabis decreased to about HK$16,083 per kilogram in 2003 as compared to average wholesale price of HK$16,396 per kilogram in 2002. The average retail price of herbal cannabis decreased slightly from HK$67 per gram in 2002 to HK$58 in 2003. The amount of cannabis resin seized increased substantially from 0.37 kilograms in 2002 to 24.46 kilograms in 2003.

Methamphetamine, in crystalline form or sometimes liquid form, is smuggled into the SAR via the land boundary with the Mainland. Whilst the vast majority is for local consumption, in a few cases foreign nationals from Asia have been apprehended when attempting to smuggle small amounts of 'ice' back to their homelands via the Hong Kong International Airport. In 2003, a total of 41.10 kilograms of methamphetamine were seized. The wholesale price of methamphetamine averaged HK$54,458 per kilogram in 2003 while the average retail price of one gram was HK$374

Cocaine, originating from South America, is smuggled into Hong Kong by couriers secreting the drug on their body or in luggage and sometimes by swallowing the drug. Another method of smuggling cocaine is to send it to the SAR by post or courier falsely declared as some innocuous item. In 2003, cocaine remained expensive with an average retail price of HK$1,152 per gram. The logistics of trafficking cocaine from distant production areas in South America to the region and consequent limited supply keep the costs high. Cocaine abuse has not been widespread in the SAR. The total cocaine seizures in 2003 amounted to 8.33 kilograms, a slight increase compared to 8.30 kilograms in 2002.

Abuse of prescription medicinal preparations continued in 2003 and seizures of midazolam (38,617 tablets), chlordiazepoxide (24,784 tablets), diazepam (22,190 tablets) and triazolam (13,165 tablets) were made. Young persons often abuse tranquillizers, however, heroin addicts also consume the tablets to prolong the effect of the narcotic and ease withdrawal symptoms. A relatively new drug of abuse to Hong Kong with the proprietary name 'Erimin 5' which contains Nimetazepam, was abused by youngsters along with other psychotropic substances in 2003.

On one occasion in 2003 a small amount of Gamma-Hydroxybutyric Acid (GHB) was seized. This was the fourth seizure of the drug in Hong Kong since it was scheduled as a dangerous drug in October 2001.

In order to interdict transnational drug trafficking the Hong Kong Police and Customs officers work closely with their counterparts in the Mainland and overseas. As a result of the close partnership with Mainland enforcement agencies, substantial seizures of drugs were made before the illicit consignments could reach lower level traffickers and abusers. Furthermore, Narcotics Bureau of the Police participated in several major international drug trafficking investigations with overseas law-enforcement agencies in 2003. Significant seizures made overseas with the assistance of Narcotics Bureau totaled 92 kgs of methamphetamine, 9.3 kgs of heroin, 800 kgs of cannabis and 12,000 ecstasy-type tablets.

Drug Trafficking Flow

As there are no significant amounts of illicit drugs grown or processed in Hong Kong, substances seized locally are for the most part smuggled into the SAR. Hong Kong has for some considerable time ceased to be a location for transit or transhipment of large consignments of drugs. The majority of substances smuggled into Hong Kong are to be sold and consumed locally.

Smuggling overland is the means by which most heroin and methamphetamine reach Hong Kong. Heroin, which is produced in the Golden Triangle, enters Mainland China via its land borders. Consignments are then carried overland to Guangdong Province where syndicates purchase some portion in order to supply the Hong Kong market. Small consignments are then smuggled across the land boundary on vehicles or by foot passengers. Methamphetamine is similarly conveyed into the territory across the land boundary.

Smuggling bulky drugs such as herbal cannabis by the sea route is a still a viable option for traffickers on account of the extensive maritime traffic in waters surrounding Hong Kong. Use of air transport for drug smuggling remains one of the preferred methods for those dealing in drugs from distant continents, including ecstasy tablets from Europe and cocaine from South America. Syndicates make use of couriers who have drugs packed on the body or concealed in luggage or on occasions have internally concealed the drugs.

DRUG ARRESTS

During 2003, 8,652 persons were arrested for drug offences, a decrease of 8.08% when compared to the 9,413 persons arrested in 2002. There were 2,827 arrests for major drug offences such as drug manufacturing or trafficking or possession of large amounts, a decrease of 6% when compared to 3,010 major drug offence arrests in 2002. The number of arrests for minor offences (e.g. possession of small amounts of drugs for own consumption) fell from 6,403 in 2002 to 5,825 in 2003.

The trend of increasing numbers of young people arrested for drug offences witnessed in 2000 and 2001 has reversed in the past two years. In 2003, a total of 474 young persons were arrested for major offences as compared to 552 the previous year. A total of 739 young people were arrested for minor drug offences, a decrease when compared to the 1,025 arrested in 2002.

Number of Persons Arrested for Drug Offences

Year	Major Drug Offences (DD)	Minor Drug Offences (DD)	Major (other drugs)	Minor (other drugs)	Total
2003	2,741	5,130	86	695	8,652

Update for 2004–to Date

There were 4,573 persons arrested for all drug offences compared to 4,182 last year; representing a 9.3% increase.

Of those persons arrested 885 (or 19.4%) were under 21-years of age compared to 623 (or 14.9%) in the preceding year.

A total 2,811 persons were arrested for psychotropic substance offences compared to 2,134 last year (+31.7%).

Of the persons arrested for psychotropic substance offences a total of 797 (or 28.4%) were under the age of 21, compared to 541 (or 25.4%) last year.

In the first 6 months of 2004 a total of 1,573 persons were arrested for ketamine-related offences, a 112% increase when compared to 742 the corresponding period last year.

Large cocaine seizures have been made in 2004 (e.g 30.08 kgs in a single case/ 5 kgs in a single case).

Drug seizures in the first half of 2004 are set out below:

	2004 (Jan-Jun)
Cocaine (kg)	44.27˜
Heroin (kg)	27.02
Cannabis Herbal (kg)	123.06
Methylamphetamine (kg)	15.11
Ecstasy-type Tablets (tab)	187,788▲
Ketamine (kg)	52.52˜

˜ 30.08 kgs seized in a single case.

▲ Several large seizures in single cases were made including one of 70,000 tablets.

˜ 14 kgs seized in a single case.

*All figures are provisional figures only.

In: Organized Crime, Gangs and Trafficking ISBN: 978-1-61122-829-8
Editors: C. Webb and P. Dobrev

Chapter 9

Hong Kong: Chinese Human Smuggling

James O. Finckenauer and Ko-Lin Chin

Definition

In law enforcement community, the terms 'human smuggling' and 'illegal migration' are used interchangeably though there is a distinct difference in their nature.

Human smuggling is commonly understood as the process in which a person physically participates for gaining illegal entry into a country. There are a variety of reasons that initiate that person to set off his illicit attempt but his final goal is no more than making a decisive intent for migration to the receiving country.

Hence, human smuggling is the prerequisite process that leads to the fulfillment of one's intent for illegal migration. Alternatively speaking, human smuggling is the means and illegal migration is the goal.

Nature

It has been well acknowledged by sociologists of different disciplines as well as policymakers in public sectors worldwide that the flow of migration, irrespective internal or international, is governed by two key elements, the push and the pull factors. Massey et al (1993) have summarized and examined the currently dominant theoretical frameworks on these push and pull factors. Some of those frameworks can be used to explain the migratory flow of Mainland Chinese to receiving countries.

The Neoclassical Economics: Macro Theory (or better known as Macroeconomic Model) (ibid, pp. 3-4) suggests that international migration is caused by the wide wage rates disparity between two countries. In the presence of the obvious wage gap between Mainland China and other affluent immigrant-receiving countries/regions such as USA, Canada, Australia Europe and Hong Kong, some individuals may seek to leave their homeland for those receiving countries with a view to making a better living. That model appears to have provided a plausible explanation to the migratory situation relating to Mainland Chinese.

Intrinsically, the push and the pull factors are materialized and co-existing at that stage.

For a high-skilled individual, his application for migration to the receiving country may not meet with obstacles and his immigration may be legitimately granted after assessment. However, for an unskilled or low-skilled individual, he may not qualify to meet the conditions laid down as immigration requirements, and such failure may lead him to resolve, if the push and pull factors are so prevailing, his dilemma by illegal means. The obvious choice is human smuggling.

Process

As mentioned earlier, human smuggling is a process involving transnational crossing. There are stakeholders playing different roles and functions in such process for profitable returns – a smuggling ring is formed. They often interact with each other throughout the process up to its completion, and then a new cycle may initiate again with new participants.

Deriving from operational experience, the stakeholders may by categorized into 6 types. Figure 1 is the organization model used to generally illustrate their distinctive roles. Their functions in the smuggling process are further illustrated in Figure 2.

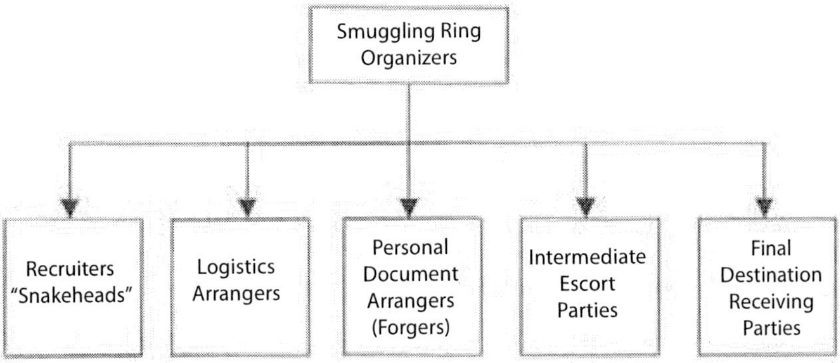

Figure 1. Organization model of smuggling ring.

In the smuggling ring, the recruiters (or commonly known as 'snakeheads') would contact the clientele (commonly known as 'illegal migrants'), or vice versa, in their homeland. After reaching an agreement with the clientele, the logistics arrangers would step in to plot out what transportation means are required to complete the whole process until the clientele are successfully transported to the receiving countries. The document arrangers would, on the other hand, arrange all the necessary documents, whether genuine or forged, for their clientele to use in the process.

The action stage commences when the clientele physically leave their homeland for the receiving countries. The smuggling ring organizers would deploy certain ring members to act as escorting parties to the clientele for ensuring the subsequent process is carried out smoothly. Circuitous routings will be designed to shaking off tracks and traces and intermediate ports of relay will be included for achieving that purpose in the whole journey.

At the final stage, the clientele will 'touch down' the receiving countries where they will be resettled, or job-hunting, and repay their debts to the ring organizers.

With reference to past investigations, the most popular receiving countries are USA, Canada, Australia, and Europe. The intermediate ports of relay are Hong Kong, major cities in Malaysia, Thailand and certain African cities like Cairo and Dubai. Figure 3 below shows the possible routings adopted by smuggling rings.

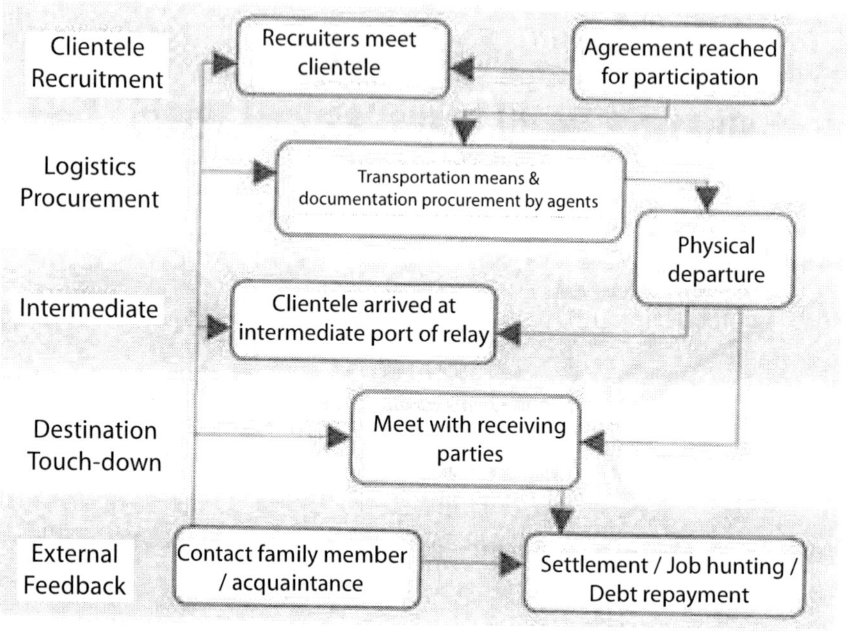

Figure 2. Process model for human smuggling.

Figure 3. Major destinations of illegal migrants.

Legislative & Administrative Measures

The common law system in Hong Kong and the statutory instruments enacted over the past decades have provided significant volume of judicial precedents (case law) and ordinances (substantive law) to deal with crimes of all nature, including those criminal offences arising in human smuggling activities. Amongst them are the Immigration Ordinance (Chapter 115), Crimes Ordinance (Chapter 200) and The Organized and Serious Crimes Ordinance (Chapter 455) of the Laws of Hong Kong. The provisions of these ordinances have provided effective enforcement and prosecutorial basis to prevent Hong Kong from being used by syndicates as a springboard for smuggling persons overseas.

Administratively, the Hong Kong Immigration Service, the Hong Kong Police Force, and the Customs and Excise Department have jointly worked in concerted efforts to prevent, detect, arrest and prosecute human smuggling offenders through frequent and regular law enforcement operations. The Hong Kong Immigration Service has also maintained close contacts with her international counterparts on intelligence sharing and exchange with respect to human smuggling activities.

Conclusion

Human smuggling activities are orchestrated by smuggling ring organizers. By nature, smuggling is the process involving transnational crossing. As illustrated earlier, different stakeholders have to be attentive in each component in the smuggling process whose operations would rely in fact upon well-established networks of interpersonal ties. In examining the Network Theory, Massey et al (1993) points out that

"[w]hen migrant networks are well-developed, they put a destination job within easy reach of most community members and make emigration a reliable and secure source of income. Thus the self-sustaining growth of networks occurs through the progressive reduction of costs may also be explained theoretically by the progressive reduction of risks."

This argument may be viewed as a plausible projection that the human smuggling activities may not be completely eliminated in view of their self-sustaining abilities. Nevertheless, through the concerted efforts exerted globally by transnational cooperation amongst concerned nations over the subject matter, the problem of human smuggling is expected to be effectively contained in a lesser magnitude of severity.

REFERENCES

Castles, S. & Miller, M.J. (2003) *The Age of Migration.* New York: Guilford Press.

Chan. J SC, & Rwezaura B. (Eds) (2004) *Immigration Law in Hong Kong-An Interdisciplinary Study*. Hong Kong: Sweet & Maxwell Asia.

Massey, D. et al. (1993) "Theory of International Migration: A Review and Appraisal". *In Population and Development Review* (Vol. 19. No. 3 (September 1993), pp.431-466)

U.S. Department of States. (June 2004) *Trafficking in Persons Report.* Washington, DC: U.S. Government Printing Office.

INDEX

C

D

E

F

G

H

I

N

O

P

R

S

T

U

V

W

Y